Recent Studies in Economic Sciences

Information Systems, Project Managements, Economics, OR and Mathematics

Recent Studies in Economic Sciences

Information Systems, Project Managements, Economics, OR and Mathematics

Edited by

Atsushi Kadoya

Hiroaki Teramoto

Hiroshima Shudo University

Volume 9 in a Series of Monographs of Contemporary Social Systems Solutions
Produced by the Faculty of Economic Sciences, Hiroshima Shudo University

Kyushu University Press

Volume 9 in a Series of Monographs of Contemporary Social Systems Solutions
Produced by Hiroshima Shudo University

ISBN978-4-7985-0229-8

Printed in Japan

Preface

Hiroshima Shudo University established the Faculty of Economic Sciences in 1977 and the Graduate School of Economic Sciences in 2001. One goal of this faculty is to unify information sciences and economics and the faculty has endeavored to make progress in the research fields of operations research, computer sciences, mathematical economics and econometrics. While the definition of economic sciences has not been established yet, our specific understanding is that the economic sciences should unite system sciences and qualitative economic analysis and construct new fields relating to the management of the international economy, the financial system, and the national economy, or environmental issues, legal policies in communication.

The Faculty of Economic Sciences is a unique academic institution. There are no other faculties titled as "economic sciences" in Japan. Basically, we pursue analyzing various issues of contemporary economies and social systems, but its uniqueness can be observed in our efforts to balance the traditional economics and information sciences as means of analytical tools.

The Faculty consists of some 30 highly qualified members, whose research interests span a wide range of topics but more or less concern quantitative analytical frameworks. Since 2005 we have been publishing our research results in a form of monographs in English, one or two volumes a year, in order to present our academic contributions to possible readers in the world.

In the past several years, members of this faculty have made plans to expand these new frontiers as follows:

1. Macro-econometric models or micro-models which contain international economics or micro-models.
2. System analysis of financial institutions and international trade.
3. Information sciences, such as network systems or information systems or theory of reliance.
4. System sciences, such as operations research and production system analysis.
5. Research on information society and social systems.
6. Legal informatics, applying information technology to legal fields and solution of legal problems in digital society.
7. Environmental Economics, researching environmental issues from the economic viewpoints.

Faculty members have undertaken joint research with the aim of constructing these new fields and to publish our new research as a monograph as follows:

Quantitative Economic Analysis, International Trade and Finance (**2005**)

Applied Economic Informatics and Systems Sciences (**2005**)

Quantitative Analysis of Modern Economy (**2007**)

System Sciences for Economics and Informatics (**2007**)

Quantitative Analysis on Contemporary Economic Issues (**2008**)

Research on Information Society and Social Systems (**2008**)

Social Systems Solutions by Legal Informatics, Economic Sciences and Computer Sciences (**2009**)

The New Viewpoints and New Solutions of Economic Sciences in the Information Society (**2010**)

Social Systems Solutions Applied by Economic Sciences and Mathematical Solutions (**2011**)

Social Systems Solutions through Economic Sciences (**2012**)

Legal Informatics, Economic Science and Mathematical Research (**2013**)

New Solutions in Legal Informatics, Economic Sciences and Mathematics (**2014**)

Contemporary Works in Economic Sciences: Legal Informatics, Economics, OR and Mathematics (**2015**)

Challenging Researches in Economic Sciences : Legal Informatics, Environmental Economics, Economics, OR and Mathematics（**2016**）

In these monographs our aim is to develop new methods and materials for constructing new fields of economics.

The authors of papers in these monographs have participate in building this new faculty and worked to develop new horizons of system sciences, information sciences, economics, economic sciences, environmental economics, computer sciences and legal informatics. We would welcome comments or suggestions in any forms.

The 2017 monograph is also entirely financed by the Faculty of Economic Sciences and is entitled under the title of "Recent Studies in Economic Sciences : Information Systems, Project Management, Economics, OR and Mathematics" edited by Atsushi Kadoya and Hiroaki Teramoto.

This book contains contributions from wide variety of research in information society, information sciences, environmental economics, economic sciences, systems approach to the economic, managerial, mathematical, environmental, and legal subjects. The focus of most articles is on the recent developments in the relevant. The set of papers in this book reflect both each theory and wide range of applications to economic and managerial models. The economic sciences is based upon an interdisciplinary education and research area of sciences economics, econometrics, statistics, information sciences, system sciences, application information sciences, operations research and legal informatics.

This book consists of seven chapters as follows:

Chapter 1 is written by Chris Czerkawski and Osamu Kurihara. The purpose of this paper is to present and contrast dominant views on the role and importance of economic wealth and prosperity according to the Christian and Buddhist teachings The doctrinal fundamentals of the Christian and Buddhist values will be discussed followed by the comparative criticism of those views.

Chapter 2 is written by Hiroyuki Dekihara and Tatsuya Iwaki. It is important to survey human behavior for analyzing human society. The aim of their research is to develop algorithms and devices for monitoring human actions. In this paper, they develop an algorithm for monitoring eye movement using wireless electroencephalogram (EEG) headset such as Emotiv. Emotiv is simplified mold, mobile and it is not expensive. These EEG recording equipment like Emotiv has a possibility becoming popular and being used in daily life. In this paper, they investigated whether Emotiv EEG headset could record electrooculogram (EOG) similar to that recorded in general EEG amplifier. In the simulation tests, the results show that their algorithm can discriminate among the eye movement with an average accuracy of about 80% in the simplified case.

Chapter 3 is written by Nan Zhang. Big data refers to the conventional software tools in a certain period to crawl the content management and the data set. Big data technology (BDT) refers to the various types of data, the ability to quickly obtain valuable information. It is suitable for big data technology, including massively parallel processing (MPP) database, data mining, distributed file system, distributed database, cloud-computing platform, the Internet, and scalable storage system. BDT can also use to compile monetary and financial statistics, especially to measure the global flow of funds (GFF). This paper is focuses on building a statistical framework for measuring GFF, explore how to use BDT to integrates the data sources, and improve the timeliness of the existing data transmission. Applying BDT to measure GFF can provide important basis for policy authorities to guard against financial risks.

Chapter 4 is written by Ryoko Wada and Yoshio Agaoka. In the paper of Kostant-Rallis, classical harmonic polynomials on $\mathbf{C}^d$ are generalized to several vector spaces from the Lie algebraic viewpoint. In their formulation, the classical case $\mathbf{C}^d$ corresponds to the real rank1 Lie algebra $so(d,1)$. In the series of papers they further investigate harmonic polynomials corresponding to remaining real rank 1 Lie algebras: $su(p,1)$, $sp(p,1)$, $f_4(-20)$, etc. In this paper they treat the case of real rank 2 Lie algebra $so(d,2)$. They settle some conjectures, which they presented in their previous paper, concerning the generators of irreducible components of harmonic polynomials for the case $so(d,2)$.

Chapter 5 is written by Setsuko Sakai and Tetsuyuki Takahama. A representative crossover in real-coded genetic algorithms is blend crossover (BLX-α). The blendcrossover, which is a two-parent crossover, has been applied to many applications, because it can be implemented easily. Also, it can realize excellent diversity because a child is generated in an extended region including two parents. However, since the child is generated for each variable independently, the performance deteriorates in a problem with strong dependency among variables. In this study, they propose an oblique crossover (OBX) where an oblique coordinate system is built from difference vectors among individuals and a blend crossover along the oblique coordinate system is performed. The oblique crossover is rotation-invariant because the distribution of individuals is rotated, the oblique coordinate system is rotated and a child is generated according to the rotated coordinate system. However, the diversity tends to be lost because the child is generated in narrow area compared with BLX-α. In this research, they study how to select a proper oblique coordinate system from difference vectors in order to improve the diversity. The effect of selecting an oblique coordinate system is shown by solving thirteen benchmark problems.

Chapter 6 is written by Yajing Liu. This paper reviews the contemporary literature on relationship banking and SMEs. She focuses particularly on how reliable information is gathered though relationship banking to help SMEs succeed in obtaining funding, which can address the financial difficulties faced by SMEs. She also examines the development of relationship banking after the global financial crisis in 2008, and how relationship banking helped SMEs deal with the crisis, thus reducing the number of defaults. Finally, she looks at how relationship banking has evolved since the financial crisis as a result of the distinct changes in two factors-information technology and the economic environment, which affected the value of soft information.

Chapter 7 is written by Tatsuo Sato. Personality is an important trait for a project manager (PM), yet it is difficult to develop effective programs for personality development. Overemphasis on the importance of PM's personality may make it difficult to develop those who work in this role. This paper discusses effective personality development of PMs and proposes a novel PM Report Card as an effective means of fostering development.

We hope that these articles provide a comprehensive yet lively and up-to-date discussion of the state-of-the-art in information society, social systems, and the relevant research fields. We believe that this book contains a coherent view of the important unifying ideas throughout the many faces of systems approach and a guide to the most significant current areas of approach. We also appreciate that this book should contribute to build the ubiquitous society in Japan. We would like to thank Hiroshima Shudo University and the Faculty of Economic Sciences for financial supports of publishing this monograph. Also we would like to take the opportunity to thank Kyushu University Press for publishing this book and for authors for their contributions.

Finally, a profound thanks goes to our families, in continuing appreciation of their support and many other contributions.

November, 2017
Atsushi Kadoya
Hiroaki Teramoto

Contents

Chapter 1

Economic Wealth and Prosperity in Christianity and Buddhism

Chris Czerkawski* and Osamu Kurihara**
*Faculty of Economic Sciences, Hiroshima Shudo University
1-1 Ozuka-Higashi 1-chome, Asaminami-ku, Hiroshima, Japan 731-3195
** Graduate School of Engineering, Hiroshima University
1-4-1 Kagamiyama, Higashi-Hiroshima City Hiroshima, Japan 739-8527

Abstract

The purpose of this paper is to present and contrast dominant views on the role and importance of economic wealth and prosperity according to the Christian and Buddhist teachings. The doctrinal fundamentals of the Christian and Buddhist values will be discussed followed by the comparative criticism of those views.

Key Words: Economic Values, Economic Ethics, Christianity, Buddhism

1. Introduction

According to the traditional Christian teachings Buddhist doctrine diverges so radically from Christian perspectives that in many ways it seems difficult to imagine any meaningful understanding between these two religions. On the other hand, some Christians who are familiar with Buddhism believe that they have found new inspirations in the Eastern religion which greatly enriched their faith. On the other hand, mutual engagement between Christians and Buddhists can lead to unexpected outcomes. If another doctrine is easily or readily absorbed by Christians it can result in purely verbal or formal understanding without the understanding of real otherness of the Buddhist culture and tradition [1]. If however the focus is on differences, as it was in official practice of Christian churches over the ages, then no real understanding is possible and the relationship between these two great religions will be based on separation and perhaps animosity. The relation is a typical gestalt phenomenon that can be evaluated in different ways, depending on whether one emphasizes the differences or the similarities.

Comparison between Christian and Buddhist views on wealth and ethics assumes that they are both some kind of doctrinal monoliths. However this is not true. Christian religion developed in many different traditions resulting in three separate institutional churches, Orthodox, Roman-Catholic and Protestant and each of those mainstreams developed numerous individual churches and each of these churches proposed its own interpretation of the holy text. The further complication is that the fundamental holy texts differ to some extend among various Christian denominations and, to a larger extend, there are differences on such key issues as the economic values and economic ethics. The discussion of economic values in Buddhism is not easier considering lack of any uniform economic doctrine, absence of any central religious authority in Buddhist world and significant differences in interpretation of Buddhist holy texts ie sutras.

Any productive and sensible comparison of views on economic values and prosperity will have to be based on strictly enforced methodological assumptions and limitations. The first and most important is that we limit our analysis to the comparison of two particular canonical texts of Christianity and Buddhism. In case of Christianity we selected the Old and New Testament, official canon of the Roman-Catholic Church, which seems to represent, at least statistically, majority of Christians. We are aware that part of the Bible here understood as Old Testament differs in many fundamental areas among Jews, Catholics, various Protestant Churches, Greek and Russian Orthodox churches and so on. The dogmas and doctrines originating from the same text also differ among various Christian churches. Different problems arise on the Buddhist side, the Theravada and Mahayana traditions, differing Pali canon and the Mahayana new sutras, then the variety of the Mahayana traditions with Vajrayana and the numerous Mahayana denominations. Japanese Buddhism with many schools starting with the Nara sects then Tendai, Shingon, Zen, Jodo Shu, Jodo Shinshu, Nichiren Shu all offer their own interpretations of ethical and social values although the differences seem minor compared with the Christian denominations. Because of those real differences in interpretations we had to choose one particular canon which would represent Buddhism – The Pali canon combined with the new Middle Way sutras. This way we try to balance two great Buddhist traditions which continue today in very peaceful co-existence if not cooperation.

In this paper, we refer to the fundamental doctrinal differences between Christianity and Buddhism only if they are in close relationship with the topic. We do not discuss practical issues related to economical values and policy-oriented problems. Similarly, we do not present the dynamics of the changes in economic ethics from historical perspective. The applications of economic doctrines in Christianity and Buddhism to individual countries and the evaluation of their usefulness to the contemporary economic trends is also beyond the scope of this article.

2. Christian Views on Wealth and Prosperity

There is an overwhelming abundance of written testimonies to the effect that wealth was not, to say the least, recommended or desired aim of Christian believer. According to St. Paul. he presents his suffering as part of the evidence that he was blessed and called by God (e.g. 2 Cor. 4:8-18; 6:3-10; 11:13-33; 12:1-10; Gal. 6:17) [2]. He once described himself "as poor, yet making many rich; as having nothing, yet possessing everything" (2 Cor. 6:10). In Ephesians, writing from prison, five times Paul mentions wealth—referring to the gospel and all its treasures. He himself was a poor prisoner deprived of many basic human necessities, but he viewed himself as being wealthy. He further elaborated on financial needs. He implied that wealth is not necessarily a sign of God's blessing, but contentment is. He said that we must "rejoice in the Lord always" (Phil 4:4). This is also the epistle that talks about the peace of God that passes all understanding (4:7). So contentment, peace, and joy characterize a truly wealthy Christian. In fact, the New Testament *seems to show wealth more as a danger than as a blessing*. It emphasized the dangers more than the desirability of wealth. Jesus set the tone for this emphasis with his statement, "How difficult it is for those who have wealth to enter the kingdom of God! For it is easier for a camel to go through the eye of a needle than for a rich person to enter the kingdom of God" (Luke

18:24-25). This statement is cited in all three synoptic Gospels. But in our modern liberal cultures how often do we hear priests repeat it today? Jesus underscores his teaching about the dangers of wealth in his parable about the rich farmer who acquired sufficient wealth to secure a comfortable retirement. He is called a "fool" at his death. Jesus explains by saying, "So is the one who lays up treasure for himself and is not rich toward God" (Luke 12:16-21). In his evangelistic call to would-be disciples to deny themselves, take up the cross, and follow him, Jesus warns, "What does it profit a man to gain the whole world and forfeit his soul?" (Mark 8:36). If we neglect this aspect of the call of Christ in our preaching of the gospel, we will be guilty of distorting the gospel just like the liberals of an earlier generation.

In Timothy 6 we find more warnings about the dangers of wealth. Paul says that it is right to want basic necessities like food and clothing: "But if we have food and clothing, with these we will be content" (1 Tim. 6:8). Beyond that necessity, wealth is not a big deal. Paul says, "But godliness with contentment is great gain, for we brought nothing into the world, and we cannot take anything out of the world" (6:6-7). It is not essential that we are rich, but it is essential that we are godly and contented. Elsewhere Paul says that he is content even while suffering: "For the sake of Christ, then, I am content with weaknesses, insults, hardships, persecutions, and calamities. For when I am weak, then I am strong" (2 Cor. 12:10). The idea of strength in weakness is another neglected biblical doctrine today. Another strong warning comes in the parable of the sower, where Jesus says about the seed sown among thorns, "The cares of the world and the deceitfulness of riches and the desires for other things enter in and choke the word, and it proves unfruitful" (Mark 4:19). These two strong warnings tell us how the desire for wealth can cause huge harm by deceiving us into giving up God's way for the way of supposed prosperity.

The prime argument for the supreme value of rejecting wealth is however the life and teachings of Jesus. He became poor so that Christians might become rich (2 Cor. 8:9). He "emptied himself, by taking the form of a servant" (Phil. 2:7). Some say that Jesus took on the curse so that we may not have to live under it, and therefore we will not suffer as he did. But in both these passages Jesus is presented to us as an example to follow. Paul even says that he desires to "share his sufferings, becoming like him in his death" (Phil. 3:10). There is a depth of oneness with Christ that we will experience only when we suffer as he did. And to us union with Christ is the greatest wealth.

The ultimate value of being poor is often emphasized in the mainstream Christian tradition. For example many of the commended followers of Jesus in the New Testament were poor. The Macedonians were heroes because they gave despite their poverty: "We want you to know, brothers, about the grace of God that has been given among the churches of Macedonia, for in a severe test of affliction, their abundance of joy and their extreme poverty have overflowed in a wealth of generosity on their part" (2 Cor. 8:1-3). The giving of these poor Christians is described using the word *wealth*. In a passage rejecting the church for considering the rich as superior to the poor, James says, "Listen, my beloved brothers, has not God chosen those who are poor in the world to be rich in faith and heirs of the kingdom, which he has promised to those who love him?" (Jas. 2:5). The poor believers were actually rich!

The sanctification of the poor is not in any way contradictory with the New Testament promise of prosperity as a blessing of faithfulness to God (e.g. Deut. 28:11). In fact, Christian Bible contains many examples of the faithful believers who lamented over their poverty contrasted with prosperity of the wicked and non-believers. This anguish could only be solved when the Christians were promised that in the Final Judgement God will impose his will and punish the sinners by everlasting suffering in hell. In this context in modern times significance of poverty and wealth for Christianity may have another interesting aspect. It seems that the greatest growth of Christian churches takes place in poor and underdeveloped countries of Africa, Asia and Latin America. On the other hand, wealthy countries of Western Europe, Australia and to some extend North America experienced a visible regress Christianity both as an institution and a moral and ethical authority.

The modern Christian doctrine on wealth and prosperity is based on Papal encyclical letters especially on historically first one, Rerum Novarum, laid by Pope Leo XIII (1891) which advocated economic distribution of wealth, criticized both capitalism and socialism, although its roots can be traced to the writings of Catholic thinkers such as Thomas Aquinas and Augustine of Hippo. Leo XIII's encyclical *Rerum novarum* in 1891 marked the beginning of the development of a systematic social teaching in the Catholic Church. It dealt with persons, systems and structures, the three co-ordinates of the modern promotion of justice and peace, now established as integral to the Church's mission. In the years which followed there have been numerous encyclicals and messages on social issues; various forms of Catholic action developed in different parts of the world; and social ethics taught in schools and seminaries. To mark the 40th anniversary of *Rerum novarum*, Pope Pius XI issued *Quadragesimo anno*, which expanded on some of its themes.

The more recent official policy on wealth and prosperity came in the post-World War II period when attention turned to the problems of social and economic development and international relations. On May 15, 1961 Pope John XXIII released *Mater et magistra*, subtitled "Christianity and Social Progress". This encyclical expanded the Church's social doctrine to cover the relations between rich and poor nations, examining the obligation of rich countries to assist poor countries while respecting their particular cultures. It includes an examination of the threat of global economic imbalances to world peace. On April 11, 1963, Pope John expanded further on this in *Pacem in terris* (Latin: *Peace on Earth*), the first encyclical addressed to both Catholics and non-Catholics. In it, the Pope linked the establishment of world peace to the laying of a foundation consisting of proper rights and responsibilities between individuals, social groups, and states from the local to the international level. He urged Catholics to understand and apply the social teachings.

Further developments came from the Second Vatican Council concerning social teachings is *Gaudium et spes*, the "Pastoral Constitution on the Church and the Modern World", which is considered one of the chief accomplishments of the Council. Unlike earlier documents, this is an expression of all the bishops, and covers a wide range of issues of the relationship of social concerns and Christian action. At its core, the document asserts the fundamental dignity of each human being, and declares the Church's solidarity with both those who suffer, and those who would comfort the suffering:

John Paul II continued his predecessors work of developing the body of Catholic social doctrine. Of particular importance were his 1981 encyclical *Laborem exercens* and *Centesimus annus* in 1991 [3]. *Laborem exercens* qualifies the teaching of private ownership in relation to the common use of goods that all men, as children of God, are entitled to. The Church has always understood this right within the broader context of the right common to all to use the goods of the whole creation: the right to private property is subordinated to the right to common use, to the fact that goods are meant for everyone. Many of these concepts are again stressed in *Centesimus annus*, issued on the occasion of the 100th anniversary of *Rerum novarum*, which includes a critique of both socialism and capitalism. Another major progress under Pope John Paul II's papacy occurred in 2005, with the publication of the Compendium of the Social Doctrine of the Church, a work entrusted to the Pontifical Council for Justice and Peace.

Pope Benedict XVI's 2009 Encyclical *Caritas in Veritate* added many additional perspectives to the Social Teaching tradition, including in particular relationships with the concepts of Charity and Truth, and introduced the idea of the need for a strong "World Political Authority" to deal with humanity's most pressing challenges and problems. This idea has proven to be controversial and difficult to accept, particularly by right-of-center U.S. Catholic thinkers who are generally suspicious, or even disdainful, of supranational and international organizations, such as the United Nations. The concept was further developed in a 2011 Note issued by the Pontifical Council for Justice and Peace entitled "Towards reforming the International Financial and Monetary Systems in the context of World Political Authority".

In *Caritas in Veritate*, Benedict also endorsed Paul VI's social encyclical *Populorum Progressio*, setting it as a new point of reference for Catholic social thought in the 21st century. Thomas D. Williams wrote that "by honoring *Populorum progressio* with the title of 'the Rerum novarum of the present age,' Benedict meant to elevate *Populorum Progressio*, conferring on it a paradigmatic status not dissimilar to that enjoyed by *Rerum novarum* throughout the twentieth century." Williams claims that the reason for this elevation is that *Populorum Progressio*, "for all its real deficiencies, effected an important conceptual shift in Catholic social thinking, by moving from the worker question (with its attendant concerns of just wages, private property, working environment, and labor associations) to the broader and richer social benchmark of integral human development [4].

Most recently, Pope Francis, in his apostolic exhortation *Evangelii gaudium*, explicitly affirmed "the right of states" to intervene in the economy to promote "the common good". He wrote:

While the earnings of a minority are growing exponentially, so too is the gap separating the majority from the prosperity enjoyed by those happy few. This imbalance is the result of ideologies which defend the absolute autonomy of the marketplace and financial speculation. Consequently, they reject the right of states, charged with vigilance for the common good, to exercise any form of control. A new tyranny is thus born, invisible and often virtual, which unilaterally and relentlessly imposes its own laws and rules [5].

Pope Francis has warned about the "idolatry of money" and wrote: *Some people continue to defend trickle-down theories which assume that economic growth, encouraged by a free market, will inevitably succeed in bringing about greater justice and inclusiveness in the world. This opinion, which has never been confirmed by the facts, expresses a crude and naïve trust in the goodness of those wielding economic power and in the sacralized workings of the prevailing economic system.* In his second encyclical, *Laudato si*, the pope lays forth a "biting critique of consumerism and irresponsible development with a plea for swift and unified global action" to combat environmental degradation and climate change [6].

With respect to climate change, some critics have argued that Pope Francis is departing from the positions of his predecessors. Daniel Schwindt observed that "some writers seem to suggest (as is common among persons who've never taken the time to read the encyclicals themselves), that Pope Francis's Laudato Si' represents some new venture on the part of the Church - a departure from its customary range of subject matter [7]. But, Schwindt argues, his attitude toward climate change is a precise continuation of the attitude of his immediate predecessor. Pope Benedict XVI had written: *The order of creation demands that a priority be given to those human activities that do not cause irreversible damage to nature, but which instead are woven into the social, cultural, and religious* [8].

Generally all recent papal encyclical letters covered a wide area of issues of social justice, human rights, and many socioeconomic issues. They can be summarized in the following points;

1. Sanctity of human life and dignity of the person
2. Call to family, community, and participation and the pursuit of the Common Good
3. Rights and responsibilities; social justice
4. Preferential option for the poor and vulnerable

5. Dignity of work
6. Solidarity and the universal destiny of the goods of the Earth
7. Care for God's creation

There were further developments in Christian tradition although not necessarily within the framework of papal guidance. Economists with Christian roots tried to introduce Christian ideas into more specific business and economic activities such as business management, human resources and finance. The latter is an interesting case which, to some extend, paralleled ideas of islamic finance and banking. The idea of Christian finance refers to banking and financial activities which came into existence several centuries ago. The activities of the Knights Templar (12th century), Mounts of Piety (in 1462) or the Apostolic Chamber attached directly to the Vatican, a number of operations of a banking nature (money loan, guarantee, etc.) or a financial nature (issuance of securities, investments were practiced, despite the earlier prohibition of usury and the Church distrust against exchange activities (as opposed to production activities).

In modern times, the Catholic banking and finance continue to be practiced through the Vatican Bank (IOR), and many Catholic lay financial players also exist, both in Germany (e.g. Pax Bank Liga Bank, Darlehenskasse DKM) or the United States of America (e.g. Catholic Family Federal Credit Union, Holy Rosary Credit Union. Many other reformed Christian actors exist (e.g. Christian Community Credit Union, Kingdom Bank). In France, if the General Union presented itself as a Catholic credit institution, and today, social finance (non-religious ethical finance) seems to have completely replaced Christian finance (e.g. Credit coopératif, Caisses de crédit municipal) [9].

As in Islamic finance, Catholic finance claims to supervise banking operations and financial activities with moral principles directly from the interpretation of Christian religious texts (Bible) and from the doctrine of the Roman Catholic Church (Treaty of Virtues and Vices, Catholic social teaching). Also, since the subprime financial crisis, it was found that the Pontifical Council for Justice and Peace often commented on financial matters. In October 2011, was published a note "Reform of the international financial system with a view toward a general public Authority" [10].

In his book "Catholic Finance" (in French: "Finance catholique"), Dr. Antoine Cuny de la Verryère presents seven principles for a Catholic finance (named "princificats"). Some of them are inspired from the principles of Islamic finance: prohibition of short-termism, prohibition of non-virtuous investment, obligation to give priority to virtuous savings, prohibition of unjust profits, obligation to share profits, obligation of transparency, and obligation of financial exemplary.

3. Buddhist Fundamentals on Economic Wealth and Prosperity

The Buddhist teachings on economics are scattered throughout the Scriptures among teachings on other subjects [11]. A teaching on mental training, for example, may include guidelines for economic activity, because in real life these things are all interconnected. Thus, if we want to find the Buddhist teachings on economics, we must extract them from teachings on other subjects.

In the sutra Anguttaranikaya (A.II. (69-70) the Buddha mentions that there are four kinds of happiness (*sukha*) derived from wealth. They are:

1)Atthisukha - The happiness of ownership.

2)Anavajjasukha - The happiness derived from wealth which is earned by means of right livelihood, i.e. not dealing in the sale of harmful weapons, not dealing in the slaughter of animals and sale of flesh, not dealing in the sale of liquor, not dealing in the sale of human beings (e.g. slavery and prostitution) and not dealing in the sale of poisons.

3)*Ananasukha* - the happiness derived from not being in debt.

4)*Bhogasukha* - the happiness of sharing one's wealth. This kind of happiness is an extremely important concept in Buddhism.

Although the Buddha saw that economic stability was important for man's happiness, he also saw the harmful side of wealth. Rather, he saw that man's natural desires and propensities are such that wealth provides ample scope for these propensities to surface and indulge themselves. Yet, it appears, desires can never be fully satisfied for it is stated in the Ratthapalasutta (M.II.68) "Uno loko atitto tanhadaso." The world is never satisfied and is ever a slave to craving. The Dhammapada (vs. 186-187) also points out this insatiability in man. "Na kahapana vassena titthi kamesu vijjati..." Not by a shower of gold coins does contentment arise in sensual pleasures.

On another occasion the Buddha said, "Grass is to be sought for by those in need of grass. Firewood is to be sought for by those in need of firewood. A cart to be sought for by those in need of a cart. A servant by him who is in need of a servant. But, Headman, in no manner whatsoever do I declare that gold and silver be accepted or sought for". The meaning is very clear from these statements. Wealth is to be sought not as an end in itself but as a means to an end, for attaining various objectives and fulfilling duties.

The Andhasutta (128-129) presents analogy where we can locate the ethically ideal position. The Buddha says there are three types of persons to be found in the world: The totally blind, the one who can see with one eye, and, the one who can see with both eyes. The man who is totally blind is the one who can neither acquire wealth nor discern right from wrong. The one who can see with one eye is the man who can acquire wealth but cannot discern right from wrong. The one who has perfect sight in both eyes is the ideal individual. He can acquire wreath and also discern what is right from wrong. The Buddhist view is that the ideal man is the man who is wealthy and virtuous.

In another analogy the Buddha classified people into the following categories:

> Tama (dark) to Tama (dark)
> Tama (dark) to Joti (light)
> Joti (light) to Tama (dark)
> Joti (light) to Joti (light)

The Tama person is poor and may or may not possess good qualities such as faith and generosity. The Joti person is rich and may or may not possess good qualities such as faith and generosity. The Tama person who does not possess good qualities who is mean and devoid of faith will go from from darkness to darkness. The Tama person who has faith and is of a generous disposition will go from darkness to light. The joti person who is devoid of faith and generosity will go from light to darkness. The Joti person who has good qualities will go from light to light. Sometimes wealth causes certain people to be miserly. The Buddha has remarked that riches "that are not rightly utilized run to waste, not to enjoyment" and compares such a person to a lake of pure water lying in an inaccessible savage region [12].

Although the Buddha never specifically taught about the subject of economics, teachings about the four requisites - food, clothing, shelter and medicine - appear throughout the Pali Canon. In essence, all of the teachings concerning the four requisites are teachings on economics.

Fundamental for Buddhism (Originally known as the Middle Way) is the wisdom of moderation. When the goal of economic activity is seen to be satisfaction of desires, economic activity is open-ended and, without clear definition, desires are endless. According to the Buddhist approach, economic activity must be controlled by the qualification that it is directed to the attainment of well-being rather than the "maximum satisfaction" sought after by traditional economic thinking. Well-being as an objective acts as a control on economic activity. No longer are we struggling against each other to satisfy endless desires. Instead, our activities are directed toward the attainment of well-being. If economic activity is directed in this way, its objectives are clear and its activities are controlled. A balance or equilibrium is achieved. There is no excess, no overconsumption or overproduction. In the classical economic model, unlimited desires are controlled by scarcity, but in the Buddhist model they are controlled by an appreciation of moderation and the objective of well-being. The resulting balance will naturally eliminate the harmful effects of uncontrolled economic activity.

The fundamentals of the Buddhist teachings on wealth and economic ethics can be summarized in the following points;

(1) Middle Way Economics: Realization of True Well-being

Buddhism is full of teachings referring to the Middle Way, the right amount and knowing moderation, and all of these terms may be considered as synonyms for the idea of balance or equilibrium. Knowing moderation is referred to in the Buddhist scriptures as *mattaññuta*. Knowing moderation means knowing the optimum amount, how much is "just right". It is an awareness of that optimum point where the enhancement of true well-being coincides with the experience of satisfaction. This optimum point, or point of balance, is attained when we experience satisfaction at having answered the need for quality of life or well-being. Consumption, for example, which is attuned to the Middle Way, must be balanced to an amount appropriate to the attainment of well-being rather than the satisfaction of desires. Thus, in contrast to the classical economic equation of maximum consumption leading to maximum satisfaction, we have moderate, or wise consumption, leading to well-being.

(2) Middle Way Economics: Not Harming Oneself or Others

A further meaning of the term "just the right amount" is of not harming oneself or others. This is another important principle and one that is used in Buddhism as the basic criterion of human action, not only in relation to consumption, but for all human activity. Here it may be noted that in Buddhism "not harming others" applies not only to human beings but to all that lives.

From a Buddhist perspective, economic principles are related to the three interconnected aspects of human existence: human beings, society and the natural environment. Buddhist economics must be in concord with the whole causal process and to do that it must have a proper relationship with all three of those areas, and they in turn must be in harmony and mutually supportive. Economic activity must take place in such a way that it doesn't harm oneself (by causing a decline in the quality of life) and does not harm others (by causing problems in society or imbalance in the environment).

From a Buddhist perspective, excessive wealth and an extravagant way of life can become a source of attachment, and create a fear of loss and of ceaseless craving. However, Buddhism does not see wealth as intrinsically evil, and does not claim that nirvana—the state of being free from suffering and the attachments that cause it—is more difficult for the wealthy to attain. On the contrary, rich people are in a privileged position to practice the virtue of generosity, and traditional Buddhism partially connects economic success in the present, to acts of charity in the past during previous lives. Wealth itself is not the problem, as long as it is attained by honest means and used for the benefit of the wider society. Some currents in the Buddhist tradition encourage charity to the monastic community in particular, in order to accumulate spiritual merit for future lives. However, Buddhism also advocates compassionate giving to the poor and the sick as a virtue in its own right. According to one account, the Buddha walked thirty miles to teach a poor person, and first made sure he was fed before focusing on spiritual matters.

The Buddhist teaching advocates detachment and ending craving whilst it censures indulgent sensual pleasures. The bodhisattva abandoned a life of luxury to seek for enlightenment and even when he attained it he continued to live without much material possessions other than the minimal requisites. Indeed, a Buddhist novice has to renounce all his worldly possessions before he is allowed to enter monkhood. Buddhist scriptures [suttas] document significant number of monks came from well off backgrounds. In addition, certain Buddhist practices might be characterized as 'ascetic', such as eating one meal a day. One might thus conclude from all this that Buddhism does not have a positive attitude towards wealth. However, this view would not be in line with the Buddhist teaching. Furthermore, there is different attitude to wealth with regards to the ordained clergy (monks and nuns) and the laity.

(3) Teachings on Poverty

In Buddhism, lay people are expected to maintain livelihood for their own, their families' and society's welfare. Basic needs must be met before one can concentrate on spiritual development. It would be difficult to develop calmness if one is not physically well or one is worrying about financial concerns. Even hunger is enough to disturb the mind to the extent that it becomes difficult to concentrate. In one sutta, the Buddha came to a village to teach a man whom he saw as capable of attaining insight. However, when he got there the man was so hungry and tired that the Buddha asked for him to be fed before delivering the discourse which helped him gain insight [10]. Elsewhere in the Scriptures the Buddha said, **'Hunger is the greatest illness'**. Similarly, one cannot have peace of mind when one is excessively worried about financial affairs, such as debts and therefore, 'for householders in the world, poverty is suffering [13].

Not only poverty does not provide people with basic needs it also does not give them as much opportunity to practice generosity and thus accumulate merit. More importantly though, poverty is also seen as one of the causes of social problems, such as crime and violence. In one sutta, the Buddha described how poverty led to social problems such as stealing, killing, lying and shortened lives For lay people therefore, poverty creates suffering both on a personal and social level; and hence for them, 'woeful in the world is poverty and debt' [14].

(4) Teachings on Wealth

In Buddhism poverty and debt is a source of suffering for a lay person. In fact, in Buddhism wealth itself is neither praised nor reproved, only how it is accumulated and used. Wealth is blameless if it is rightfully obtained, without hurting others, i.e., without violence, stealing, lying and deception. This is Right Livelihood and it is one of the factors of the Noble Eightfold Path (the Buddhist Path). Thus, wrong livelihood would include trades which involve killing, directly and indirectly such as butchery and trading in arms respectively. It also includes trades which involve frauds and deception. Even marketing is considered wrong livelihood to the extent that more often than not involves a certain amount of deception (making the products more appealing than what it is) and also it draws on people's aspirations, prejudices and desires (Payutto, 1994). On a more subtle note, even right livelihood can sometimes be considered wrong if it is practiced with the wrong motivation, for example a doctor who recommends medicine that is not really necessary for the patient's condition.

Buddhist Scriptures introduced the notion of being **'two eyed'** when it comes to making a living. One has to keep one eye on profit and the other on ethics. According to the Scriptures, there are three kinds of people in the world: they are the blind, the one-eyed and the two-eyed. The blind person does not know how to generate wealth, does not know what is right and wrong, and does not know what is good and bad. This person has no wealth and cannot perform good works (such as giving gifts, making donations, etc). The one-eyed person knows how to generate wealth but does not know what is blameworthy or not, and what is good or evil. This person may thus obtain wealth through whatever means including violence, theft and deception. Though he/she enjoys sense pleasures from the wealth generated, when he/she dies is reborn in hell. The two-eyed person knows how to generate wealth, but also knows what is right and wrong, blameworthy or not, and whether it is good or evil. This person enjoys his/her wealth in this life but also after death is reborn to a good destination [15].

(5) Wealth as a Virtue

Though it is traditionally thought that wealth can be the result of a good rebirth, a karmic consequence of generosity, other factors contribute towards financial success and happiness are:

1. Industriousness - energetic striving in one's job.
2. Watchfulness - taking care of one's property to prevent lost due to robberies and natural disasters such as flood.
3. Having good friends - so one can emulate their actions.
4. Leading a balanced life - one does not spend excessively nor hoards wealth.

On the other hand, the virtues of wealth can be vastly diminished by:

1. Addiction to drink/drugs.
2. Haunting the streets at night - leaving one's property unprotected.
3. Addiction to entertainments and amusements and always on the look out for them.
4. Addiction to gambling.
5. Keeping bad company such as gamblers, drunks and fraudsters.
6. Habitual idleness - one is too lazy to do anything [16].

In the official Pali Canon there are numerous examples of virtuous behavior recommended to the lay men.

In the Anguttaranikaya (A III 279) the Buddha says that there are five advantages to be gained in having wealth. With one's wealth one can make oneself, parents, wife, children, workers, friends and colleagues happy and also make offerings to recluses and Brahmins. The Buddha says that a person who spends his money in this way can be compared to a lovely lake with clear, blue, cold, delicious, crystalline water which lies near a village or township from which people can draw water, drink from it, bathe in it and use it for any other purpose. (S. I.90) The Pattakammasutta (A II 67) extends this list besides the above ways of spending money to include securing wealth against misfortunes by way of fire, water, king, robbers, enemies or ill disposed heirs, spending wealth for the fivefold offerings such as natibali (relatives), atithibali (guests), petabali (departed ancestors) rajabali (king's tax) devabali (gods), and offering gifts to recluses and Brahmins who abstain from sloth and negligence who are genuinely disciplined, kind and forbearing.

The Pattakammasutta goes on to say that if a person disregarding these fourfold purposes spends his money it is called "wealth that has failed to seize its opportunity, failed to win merit, unfittingly made use of."

Buddhist ethics are based on the principle that certain actions (kamma) result in certain effects; in short, they are based on the Law of Causality - Paticcasamupada. But, we may ask, why do immoral acts result in suffering and unhappiness? What is the correlation between moral acts and beneficial results?

The Buddha's prescription for prosperity and happiness in this and in the next life is based on very practical advice of a worldly nature, inextricably linked with ethics. The layman's code of ethics - which includes the observance of the pancasila - the five precepts - is a sine qua non for all Buddhists. The social consequences of observing the basic ethics enunciated in the layman's code of ethics are very extensive. They contribute to producing a protective atmosphere of security and goodwill around one which is conducive to both material and spiritual progress [17].

Some authors believe that Buddha's thoughts in happiness as pessimistic because it claims that humans desire in this world will only lead to suffering. However, such claim is only true in a condition that the Buddhist did not have strong spirituality in life. If the spirituality aspect is taken into account, a view on happiness in the Buddha teaching will be changed. The first view only depends on the unbalanced emotional states of the mind. However, in a deeper way, Buddhists actually can experience a true happiness by spiritual activity. Wiist, Sullivan, Wayment, and Warren (2010) found a strong relation between years of practicing Buddhism and spending more time in a typical meditative session and rituals with a psychological mindfulness, which is a source of being happy. In addition, a true happiness can also be found when one avoids a selfish behavior, not looking their self as "me" or "mine" in their action. As written by Rahula (1974) cited in Gaskins (1999) [18].

This is also supported by Payutto (1994) who stated that enlightenment in Buddhism cannot be reached without freedom of all selfishness (*Arahant*) both internally and externally. Therefore, Buddhists are encouraged to practice a constructive behavior among themselves as the way to find virtue and truth (*dhamma*; Payutto, 1994) and the way to the enlightenment (*nirvana*). Achieving the highest happiness (*nibbana*) for Buddhists through the enlightenment is a long process and gradually Buddhist practitioners have to go through an awakening process. Starting from building basic kindness, generosity must be practiced in their self before the virtue can take place in their action. With that type of combination of kindness, Buddhists have a chance to get rebirth in heaven although in time, this will make them realize it is merely a temporary happiness (rebirth happened because people cannot purse what they want in the past life). This final stage will make them start realizing that only renunciation will lead to unconditional happiness. Thus, for Buddhists, the experience gained through the gradual process has made them able to reach the happiness suggested in the Noble Path in the Buddha's teachings.

4. Buddhist Concept of Economic Values Contrasted with the Western Way

On the most general level there are deep differences between Christianity and Buddhism with regard to the supreme value of achieving wealth and prosperity leading to human happiness. Although there are some moral and ethical parallels, Christian views have roots in Judaism and Buddhist originated from Braminic Hinduism. (see table below).

With regard to more particular aspects the differences between Christianity and Buddhism can be presented as follows.

While Western economics concentrates on self-interest, the Buddhist view challenges it by changing the concept of self to *Anatta* or no-self. It says that all things perceived by one's senses are not actually "I" or "mine" and therefore, humans must detach themselves from this feeling. They believe that the self-interest based, opportunistic approach to ethics will always fail. Generosity will work because human beings are *homines reciprocantes* who tend to reciprocate to feelings (either positively or negatively) by giving back more than what is given to them.

Table 1. Various Ways to Achieve Prosperity and Happiness

Religion	Common Ways	Differences
Christianity	Doing good deeds	Wealth and Prosperity are gifts from God Creator
Buddhism	Taking the Middle Way between extremes, poverty and material wealth	Renounce desires and pleasures according to the Four Noble Paths
Judaism		Torah, book of Law teaches about wealth and happiness
Hinduism		Wealth and happiness comes from the understanding the Law of Karma, Artha, Moksha and Dharma. Proper balance with the four values recommended.
Islam		Quran and Haditha set the rules for wealth and happiness which generally can be achieved in after-life.

Western economists give importance to maximizing profits and individual gains while the underlying principle of Buddhist economists is to minimize suffering (losses) for all living or non living things. Buddhist generally believe that human beings show greater sensitivity to loss than to gains and therefore people should concentrate more on reducing the former.

There is an important difference with respect to the concept of desire. Western economic ethics encourages material wealth and desire because of which people try to accumulate more and more wealth—sometimes at the cost of others—to satisfy those cravings. In contrast, in Buddhist economics, importance is given to simplify one's desires. According to them, apart from the basic necessities like food, shelter, clothing, and medicines, other materialistic needs should be minimized. Wanting less will benefit the person, the community they live in, and the nature.

Views on the market are also different. While Western economists with Christian roots often advocate maximizing markets to a point of saturation, Buddhist economists aim at minimizing violence. According to them, Western economists do not take into consideration "primordial stakeholders" like the future generations and the natural world because their vote is not considered important in terms of purchasing power. They think that other stakeholders such as poor and marginalized people are under-represented because of their inadequate purchasing power and preference is given to the strongest stakeholder. Therefore, they believe that the market is not an unbiased place, truly representative of the economy. Thus, Buddhist economists advocate ahimsa or non-violence. According to them, *ahimsa* prevents doing anything that directly causes suffering to oneself or others and urges to find solutions in a participatory way. Community supported agriculture is one such example of community-based economic activities as it builds up trust, helps build value based communities and brings people closer to the land and the farm. Achieving this sustainability and non-violence requires restructuring of dominating configurations of modern business, which they advocate. This leads to de-emphasizing profit maximization as the ultimate motive and renewed emphasis on introducing small-scale, locally adaptable, substantive economic activities.

Western economists try to maximize instrumental use where the value of any entity is determined by its marginal contribution to the production output while Buddhist economists feel that the real value of an entity is neither realized nor given importance to. They try to reduce instrumental use and form caring organizations which will be rewarded in terms of trust among the management, co-workers, and employees.

In contrast to Buddhist economists Western economists tend to believe that bigger is better and more is more, whereas Buddhist economists believe that small is beautiful and less is more. Consequently Western economics gives importance to gross national product whereas Buddhist economics gives importance to gross national happiness [19].

Having contrasted Buddhist economic principles with the dominant market economy principles may provide useful platform for presentation of criticism of the official Christian teaching on economic wealth and economics. The underlying rationale for this criticism is determined by extensive involvement of Christians in the determination of what is right/or wrong with economic values. Buddhists, on the other hand, do not offer specific recommendations or guidelines with regard to specific economic activities.

The general criticism is that the approach found in many of the encyclicals has led the Catholic Church to attempt to impose on the economic order principles external to the science of economics, and thus, it promotes policies that are not, most probably, to be successful. The principles of economic activity are usually orderly and generally unchanging, and attempts to impose particular policies from outside of that system reflect a lack of comprehension or recognition of the reality of the economic order. In contrast Buddhist ethics tend to be more moderate and remain in line with the so-called natural order of nature.

To make this point more clear one has to state that there are certain activities in the sphere of economics that should be rejected or even condemned Fraud, theft, and malicious failure to meet contractual obligations are crimes that merit the condemnation of the moral theologian. One can agree when the Church expresses views regarding the material well-being of families and suggests that morally licit methods of improving it should be pursued. However when the Church recommends the best or most effective way to carry out that intention via minimum wages, various mandated benefits, heavy taxation on the wealthy, or whatever it is entering a field in which these conclusions must be evaluated not on the basis of its authority as a moral force but instead on the rigor of the argument.

If the Church possessed some special insight into economics merely by virtue of its transcedental authority, why not into other disciplines as well? Why should this special insight not extend, say, to medicine? As soon as we thus extend it, however, we see the logical problem with applying moral analysis to a value-neutral, scientific discipline. It is certainly quite acceptable to say, for example, that medical doctors should care about the patients, but it is quite another to employ a moralistic idiom to pronounce upon what kind of medicine should be applied to a sick person. These questions are obviously well outside the legitimate province of the moral theologian.

Another point is the issue of worker's rights. Although in his encyclical *Longinqua Oceani* (1895) Pope Leo XIII appeared to endorse only voluntary unionism rather than the coercive variety with which Western nations are intimately familiar, individual bishops, theologians, and lay defenders of the Church's social teaching often fail to make such a distinction, taking it for granted that a Catholic's support for the interests of labor includes endorsing the various special privileges that labor unions presently enjoy under the law. In short, hardly anyone who claims to speak for the Church on economic matters calls for a completely free labor market today.

In fact, there is a sound theoretical argument and of empirical evidence that coercive labor unionism makes some workers worse off; Richard Vedder and Lowell Gallaway of Ohio University have also shown that labor taken collectively is much worse off than it would have been had a free labor market prevailed over the past half century. To be sure, that conclusion appears to contradict the implied conclusion of Catholic social teaching that labor unionism is a legitimate means for workers to advance their interests, and one that Catholics should favor [20].

Pope Pius XI made a significant concession in his encyclical *Quadragesimo Anno* (1931), which marked the fortieth anniversary of the issuance of Leo XIII's seminal *Rerum Novarum*. He acknowledged that limits must exist to what the moral theologian may legitimately say within the economic sphere, since "economics and moral science employs each its own principles in its own sphere." To be sure, the Pope then went on to deny that "the economic and moral orders are so distinct from and alien to each other that the former depends in no way on the latter." But once it has been conceded that economics is a bona fide science possessing an internal coherence of its own, problems immediately arise for those who would claim that Catholic social teaching definitively settles all major economic matters in an absolute and binding way. As A.M.C. Waterman points out, this concession by Pius XI "throws doubt on the authoritative character of that very substantial part of Catholic (or at least papal) social teaching which consists not of theological and ethical pronouncements, but of empirical judgments about the economy" [21].

This is the fundamental issue, as yet unresolved, in Catholic social teaching from the perspective of the supporter of the market. The moral argument advanced in favor of such teachings as the "living wage" is obviously dependent on certain economic preconceptions. But if those economic preconceptions are incorrect, what happens to the moral analysis whose conclusions are based on them? For instance, churchmen have wanted to increase the material well-being of workers, and some have not ruled out the imposition of a government-mandated "living wage" in order to do so. But what if such legislation increases unemployment? Should this not be a factor in our moral evaluation of living-wage legislation? Furthermore, what if we can show that real wages are reliably increased across the board not by intrusive legislation but by an economic order that leaves capital accumulation unhampered, thereby increasing the productivity of labor? Facts like these must inform our judgment of such important matters.

The process by which the free market leads to an ever-higher standard of living occurs without having to threaten violence against anyone or to confiscate anyone's wealth by force. It certainly occurs very much in spite of destructive campaigns for a "living wage" often, in the name of Catholic social teaching which fail to understand how this process occurs and which only make it more expensive to hire people in the first place. Labor and capital alike should want the same thing: an economic environment with as little taxation as possible (even none at all), and an environment in which business investment and expansion are unhampered. How could this conclusion not be central to sound and sensible moral reasoning?

Most people, including Catholic commentators, take for granted that the government must enact legislation governing working conditions. Now certainly the popes would oppose state-mandated safety requirements so stringent as to cause serious disruption in employment. As free-market economists have suggested, however, there is only one non-arbitrary way of ensuring that increases in working conditions do not come at the expense of other goods that society at large as well as workers themselves value more highly. That way involves market exchange. For that reason, therefore, there is nothing subversive or objectionable taking place when a Catholic recommends the market as the best way of implementing the popes' concern for working conditions, even if this particular solution may not have occurred to them (as indeed it does not occur to most people).

Another criticism refers to more controversial issue ie the problem of child labor, which remains the source of a great deal of moralizing. Far from a product of the Industrial Revolution, child labor has existed since the beginning of time. When the productivity of labor is hopelessly low, parents naturally think of children as economic actors who can contribute to the well-being of their families. Without their children's participation in the family's work, the entire household could suffer terrible privation. This is a fact of life in poor, low-productivity societies that no "progressive" legislation can wish away [22].

Certainly, the economic sciences do not explain all ethical problems of the contemporary market economy. They do, however, show the morally acceptable desire for profit leads to spontaneous social cooperation that reduces the need for a interventionist state apparatus to direct production. It shows mechanisms by which peaceful social cooperation, without the initiation of physical force, may lead to overall prosperity. This can also mean less disease, more leisure time to spend with our families, and greater opportunities to enjoy the good things of civilization. In this respect Buddhist ethical teachings on wealth and prosperity seem to be much more in line with both natural order of nature and the fundamentals of liberal economy and the free market [23]. (Morality and Economic Law: Toward a Reconciliation (By Tom Woods).

References

[1] Knitter Paul, Without Buddha I cannot be a Christian, Paperback, Summer Reading 2013

[2] All quotes after the official New Testament of the Roman-Catholic Church.

[3] In Evangelum Vitae, par 18, *On one hand there is a growing moral sensitivity alert to the value of every individual as a human being without any distinction of race, nationality, religion, political opinion, or social class. On the other hand these proclamations are contradicted in practice. How can these solemn affirmations be reconciled with the widespread attacks on human life and the refusal to accept those who are weak, needy, elderly, or just conceived? These attacks go directly against respect for life; they threaten the very meaning of democratic coexistence, and our cities risk becoming societies of people who are rejected, marginalized, uprooted, and oppressed, instead of communities of "people living together."* Laborem Execrens and *Centesimus Annus,* available on the official Vatican site

[4] Thomas D. Williams, *The World as it Could Be: Catholic Social Thought for a New Generation* (New York: Crossroad, 2011):173-74

[5] see http://w2.vatican.va/content/francesco/en/apost_exhortations/documents/papa-francesco_esortazione-ap_20131124_evangelii-gaudium.html

[6] Jim Yardley & Laurie Goodstein, Pope Francis, in Sweeping Encyclical, Calls for Swift Action on Climate Change, *New York Times* (June 18, 2015).

[7] Daniel Schwindt, Catholic Social Teaching: A New Synthesis (Rerum Novarum to Laudato Si), 2015.

[8] Daniel Schwindt, 2015. op.cit.

[9] *Christoph Berndorff; Gerd Greven; Winfried Hinzen. "Bank of Church and Caritas". Pax-Bank. Retrieved 2016-06-10.; "Privatkunden - LIGA Bank eG". Ligabank.de. Retrieved 2016-06-10. "Catholic Family Federal Credit Union – Home". Cffcu.com. Retrieved 2016-06-10. "Holy Rosary Credit Union". Hrcu.org. Retrieved 2016-06-10. "Kingdom Bank". Kingdom Bank. Retrieved 2016-06-10. A.R. Cuny de la Verryère, Finance catholique, edit. EMS, 2013.*

[10] In his book "Catholic Finance" (in French: "Finance catholique"), Dr. Antoine Cuny de la Verryère presents seven principles for a Catholic finance (named "princificats"). Some of them are inspired from the principles of Islamic finance: prohibition of short-termism, prohibition of non-virtuous investment, obligation to give priority to virtuous savings, prohibition of unjust profits, obligation to share profits, obligation of transparency, and obligation of financial exemplary. A.R. Cuny de la Verryère, Finance catholique, edit. EMS, 2013

[11] Payutto, Ven. P. A. "Buddhist Economics - A Middle Way for the Market Place", many editions. All quotes in this section come from the official Pali Canon of Sutras. *translated by 3.Dhammavijaya and Bruce Evans, 1994,*
http://www.geocities.com/Athens/Academy/9280/econ.htm#Contents. Lily de Silva, 'Livelihood and Development', part of her *One Foot in theWorld:*
http://www.accesstoinsight.org/lib/bps/wheels/wheel337.html#dev

[12] Mavis Fenn, Two Notions of Poverty in the Pali Canon, *Journal of Buddhist Ethics*, Vol.3 (1996),pp.98125:http://jbe.gold.ac.uk/3/fenn1.pdf. Dhammapada. A.III.262-3 as cited in Payutto, 1994

[13] Digha Nikaya, III.65-70; also Walshe, 1987: 398-401

[14] Digha Nikaya.III.189; and Walshe, 1987:466

[15] Alavakasutta and Dhananjanisutta in ;Prosperity and Happiness The Buddhist View, *Suvimalee Karunaratne Buddhist Cultural Centre, Sri Lanka,* srilankabuddhism.com

[16] Zsolnai, Laszlo. *"Buddhist Economics for Business"*, Payutto, P. A. *"Buddhist Economics - A Middle Way for the Market Place"*, also Schumacher, E. F. "BUDDHIST ECONOMICS", Anthony Blond Ltd., London, 1966

[17] The most important suttas included in the layman's code of ethics are the Mahamangalasutta, Dhammikasutta, Parabhavasutta and Vasala sutta of the Sutta nipata, the Sigalovadasutta of the Digha nikaya and Vyaggapajjasutta and the Gihisukhasutta of the Anguttaranikaya.

[18] W. Rahula, What Buddha Thought, Grove Press 1974; Heidi A. Wayment, Bill Wiist, Bruce M. Sullivan, Meghan A. Warren, Doing and Being, Mindfulness, Health and Quiet Ego Characteristics Among Buddhist Practictioners, *Journal of Happiness Studies*, Vol. 12, 2011

[19] Ven. P. A. Payutto. *Buddhist Economics - A Middle Way for the market place, translated by Dhammavijaya and Bruce Evans, 1994,*
http://www.geocities.com/Athens/Academy/9280/econ.htm#Contents; Mavis Fenn, Two Notions of Poverty in the Pali Canon, *Journal of Buddhist Ethics*, Vol.3 (1996).

[20] Richard Vedder and Lowell Gallaway, The Minimum Wage and Poverty among Full-time Workers, *Journal of labor Research*, March 2002, Vol 23.

[21] Mann S. (2007). Comparing interpersonal comparisons in utility theory and happiness research. Forum for Social Economic, 36. Also Larrimore M. (2010). Religion and the promise of happiness. Social Research, 77. Rerum Novarum § 22; Quadragesimo Anno § 5; Centesimus annus § 3.

[22] As Anna Krueger writes, "The issue of child labor is vexing: there are legitimate issues of intolerable working conditions, but employment of children may provide food that prevents a family from starving. In some instances, also, it may provide girls with an alternative to forced early marriages." Even the International Labor Organization conceded in a 1997 report, "Poverty, however, emerges as the most compelling reason why children work. Poor households need the money, and children commonly contribute around 20 to 25 percent of family income. Since by definition poor households spend the bulk of their income on food, it is clear that the income

provided by working children is critical to their survival." A. Krueger, The Church and the Market; A catholic Fefense of the Free Market, Thomas Woods Ed., 1996

[23] For views of Catholic economist on dominant Church's teachings see T. Woods, Morality and Economic Law: Toward a Reconciliation, Presented at Austrian Scholar Conference, 8 March 2002, Ludwig von Mises Institute, Auburn, Alabama.

Chapter 2

Development of an Algorithm for Monitoring Eye Movement Using Wireless EEG Headset

Hiroyuki Dekihara * *and Tatsuya Iwaki* **

* Hiroshima Shudo University, Faculty of Economic Sciences

1-1-1, Ozuka-higashi, Asaminami-ku, Hiroshima 731-3195, Japan

** Hiroshima International University, Faculty of Rehabilitation

555-36, Kurosegakuendai, Higashihiroshima City, Hiroshima, 739-2695, Japan

Abstract

In this paper, we have developed an algorithm for monitoring eye movement using wireless electroencephalogram headset such as Emotiv Epoc Premium. Our algorithm consists of four parts which are training data, input data, analyzer and classifier. The training data is EOG data for training the characteristic wave. The input data is EOG data for monitoring eye movement. The analyzer is multiple discriminant analysis. Finally, the classifier is based on the multiple discriminant analysis and is extended for applying to Emotiv Epoc Premium. The multiple discriminant classifier determines the directions of eye movement (up, down, right and left in the simplified case) by the input data. In the simulation tests, the results showed that our algorithm could correctly discriminate among the eye movement with an average accuracy of about 90% in the simplified case.

Key Words: Eye movement, Wireless EEG headset, Discriminant analysis

1. Introduction

It is important to survey human behavior for analyzing human society and human interface[1-3]. Recently, the many devices and interfaces are developed using electroencephalogram (EEG) and electrooculogram (EOG)[4-9]. The aim of our research is to develop algorithms and devices for monitoring human actions. In this paper, we have developed an algorithm for monitoring eye movement using wireless EEG headset such as Emotiv Epoc Premium (Emotiv headset). The Emotiv headset is simplified mold, mobile and it is not expensive[10]. These EEG recording equipment like the Emotiv headset has a possibility becoming popular and being used in daily life. In this paper, we investigated whether the Emotiv EEG headset could record EOG similar to that recorded in general EEG amplifier in the laboratory. Participants gazed on the fixation point at the center of screen and moved rapidly their eyes to the one of 8 directions when a figure was presented around the fixation point. EOG was recorded in these trials, then, we compared the records of this equipment and realized the characteristic EOG corresponding to eye movement. We were able to recognize the characteristic EOG wave and have developed the algorithm for our wireless human computer interface based on it. Our algorithm consists of four parts which are training data, input data, analyzer and classifier. The training data is EOG data for training the characteristic wave. The input data is EOG data for monitoring eye movement. The analyzer is multiple discriminant analysis. Finally, the classifier is based on the multiple discriminant analysis and is extended for applying to the Emotiv headset. The multiple discriminant classifier determines the directions of eye movement (up, down, right and left in the simplified case) by the input data. In the simulation tests, the results show that our algorithm could discriminate among the eye movement with an average accuracy of about 90% in the simplified case.

2.   The Pre-experimental Test

In the pre-experimental test, we examined whether the Emotiv headset was able to record EOG similar to that recorded in general EEG amplifier before developing the algorithm for monitoring eye movement.

The conditions of the pre-experimental test are described below. Participants were 3 males who were university students, attached 4 electrodes on their around parts of eyes (Above-, Below-, Right-, and Left- sides). In the pre-experimental test, the participant sat on a chair in the shield room and instructed to capture targets appearing on a display place 1m ahead by capturing their gazes (Figure 1). The target was a figure displayed around the gazing point, and it was presented to any one of the eight directions including up, down, left, right, and oblique directions (viewing angle of 11.5 degrees).

The participants stared at the center gazing point for the first time, moved the gaze according to the target appearing three seconds later, and instantly took place in accordance with the timing at which the target temporarily disappeared. With this procedure as one trial, 16 sessions (8 directions × 2 times) were taken as one session. Participants participated in 2 sessions, and carried out a total of 32 gaze movements. After the session ended, we asked for an odd number included in the number that appeared as a trigger and raised the attention to the target. Also, before practicing the session, practice trials were set.

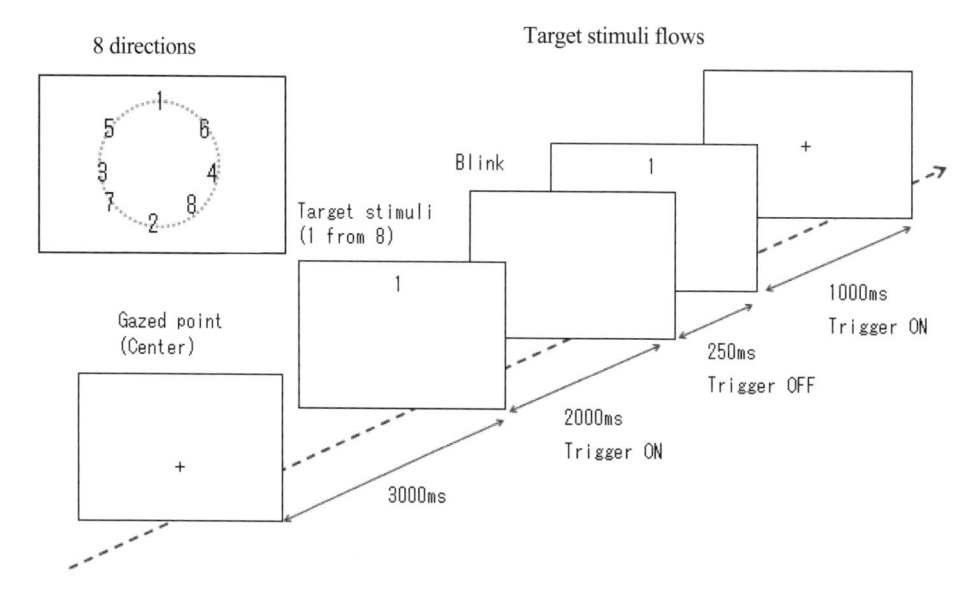

Figure 1.   Targets location and EOG recording paradigm

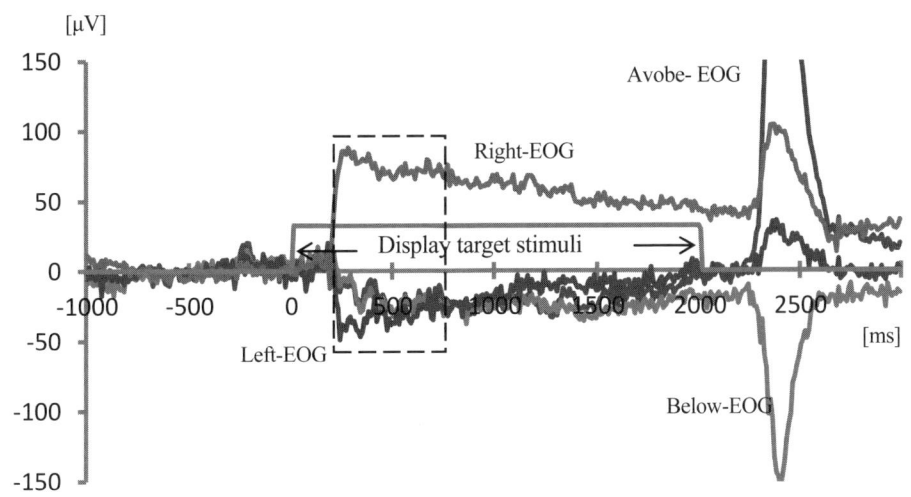

Figure 2. Example of recording EOGs in one trial

They gazed on the fixation point at the center of screen and moved rapidly their eyes to the one of 8 directions when a figure was presented around the fixation point. EOG was recorded in these trials, then, we compared the records of this equipment and realized the characteristic EOG corresponding to eye movement. We were able to recognize the characteristic EOG wave and have developed the algorithm for our wireless human computer interface based on it.

Figure 2 shows an example of recording of the EOG in one trial. The target hit the position "4" on the right side in the horizontal direction. A sharp eye potential change is seen at about 200 ms after the target is displayed. In this example, the potential of the right external eye angle rises the plus, and the left external eye angle changes to the minus. It is understood that the eye potential in the vertical direction is also changed, but the potential change is gentle, and thereafter, a large change occurs at the time of the eye blinking.

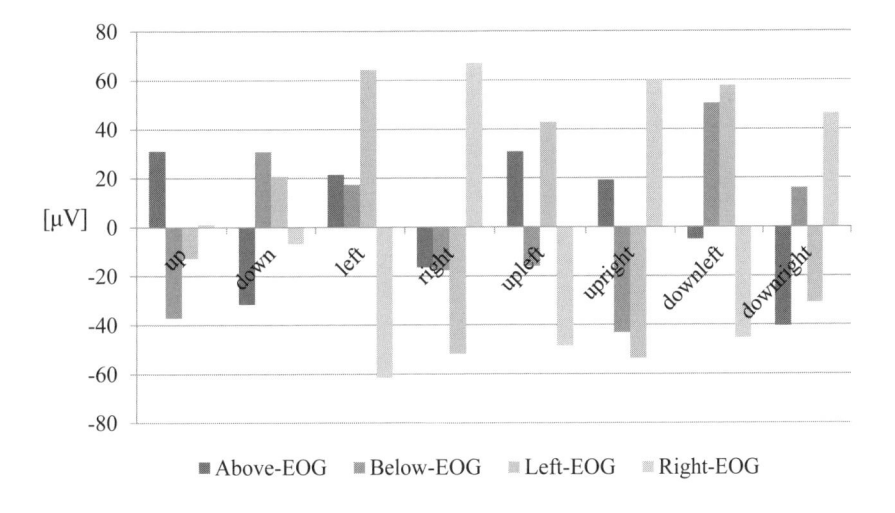

Figure 3. Averages of recording EOG every directions

In order to grasp the eye movements accompanying the movement of the glance, we extract the EOG waves from 300 ms to 450 ms after the target presentation. In Figure 3, for example, in the case of the up direction in the eye movement, the Above-EOG is plus and the Below-EOG is minus on the opposite, there is no significant change in the waves of the Right-EOG and Left-EOG. In the cases of the right and left directions in the eye movement, the potentials change in the plus according to the direction-sides. We could consider that it is able to express by the combination of the cases where the potential in the line of sight direction is plus in the case of diagonal as well. Since the electrodes attached to the above, below, left and right on the around the eyes are variable opposite in polarity depending on the direction of the target, the electrode can be handled by either one. Therefore, it is thought that even a simple headset like the Emotiv headset can be detected sufficiently.

3. The Developed Algorithm

The Emotiv headset is one of the popular EEG headsets that is able to investigate the brain waves and to connect to PC by wireless. In this section, we introduce overviews and specifications of The Emotiv headset. After that, our algorithm is described.

3.1   The Emotiv Headset

Figure 4 shows an overview of the Emotiv headset. In Figure 4, (a) is the design of the Emotiv headset and (b) is a view of the Emotiv headset mounting on a human head. The Emotiv headset has 14 electrodes with gold-plated connectors offer optimal positioning for accurate spatial resolution. The electrodes locate on AF3, F7, F3, FC5, T7, P7, O1, O2, P8, T8, FC6, F4, F8, AF4 based on the International 10–20 system. Figure 5 (a) illustrates locations of electrode of the Emotiv headset and Figure 5 (b) shows an example of recording EOG by a sample application of Emotiv using the Emotiv headset. And the list of the Emotiv headset features is shown in Table 1. The Emotiv headset has gyroscope, high performance wireless, is a dongle of USB compatible, requires no custom drives. And the lithium battery provides 12 hours of continuous use.

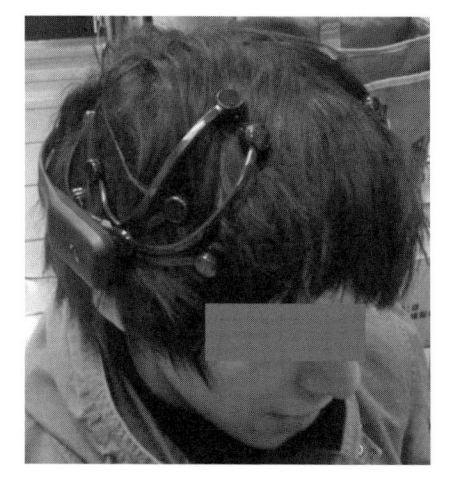

(a) Design   (b) Mounted on human head

Figure 4.   Overviews of the Emotiv headset

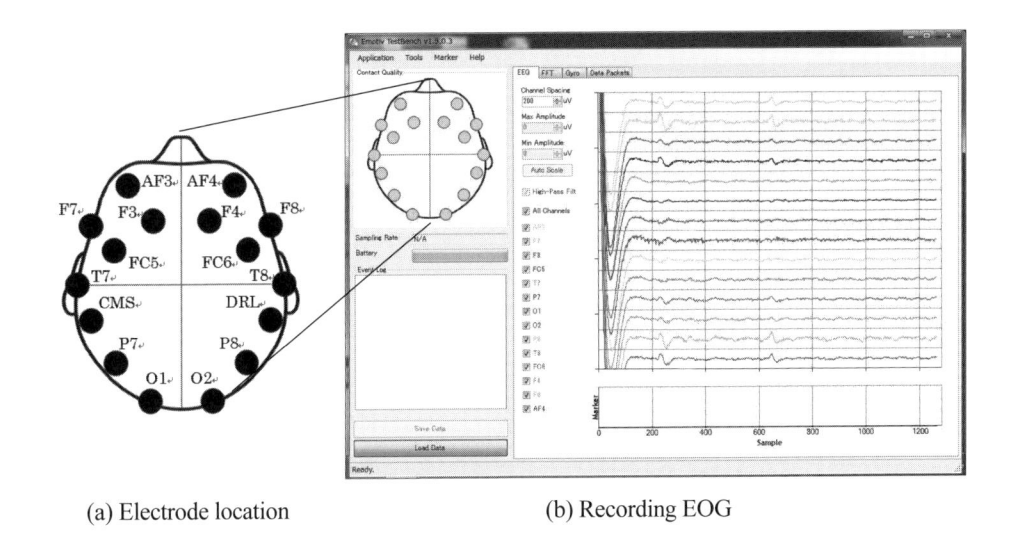

(a) Electrode location   (b) Recording EOG

Figure 5. Electrode location and example of recording EOG

Table 1. The Emotiv headset features

Machine	Average loading & unloading time
Number of channels	14 (plus CMS/DRL references, P3/P4 locations)
Channel names	AF3, F7, F3, FC5, T7, P7, O1, O2, P8, T8, FC6, F4, F8, AF4
Sampling method	Sequential sampling. Single ADC
Sampling rate	128 SPS (2048 Hz internal)
Resolution	14 bits 1 LSB = 0.51µV (16 bit ADC, 2 bits instrumental noise floor discarded)
Bandwidth	0.2 - 45Hz, digital notch filters at 50Hz and 60Hz
Filtering	Built in digital 5th order Sinc filter
Dynamic range (input referred)	8400µV (pp)
Coupling	AC coupled
Connectivity	Proprietary wireless, 2.4GHz band
Power	LiPoly
Battery life (typical)	12 hours
Impedance Measurement	Real-time contact quality using patented system

- Training Process
  ① Record electroocculogram (EOG)
    ✧ Training data
  ② Build analyzer from Training data
    ✧ based on the multiple discriminant analysis
- Running Process
  ① Record electroocculogram (EOG)
    ✧ Input data

  ② Decide direction by classifier
    ✧ Classifier based on analyzer
  ③ Control
    ✧ mouse cursor, machine, etc

Figure 6.   Scheme of monitoring algorithm

3.2   The Scheme of Our Algorithm

We have developed the algorithm monitoring eye movement for devices like human interface. Figure 6 shows a scheme of our algorithm flow. Our algorithm consists of four parts which are training data, input data, analyzer and classifier. The training data is EOG data for training the characteristic wave. The input data is EOG data for controlling mouse cursor, machine, PC, etc simultaneously with eye movement. The analyzer is multiple discriminant analysis. Finally, the classifier is based on the multiple discriminant analysis extended the Fisher's linear discriminant[11], and is extended for applying to the Emotiv headset.

In Figure 6, there are two processes: Training process and Running Process. The former is pre-set of monitoring eye movement and the latter is running the monitoring system. In the training process, the potentials of eye movements (up, down, right, left) are investigated by the Emotiv headset. And, we modified training data; selecting 4 channels (AF3, AF4, R7, R8), performing the high-pass and the low-pass filtering, calculating deviations, and extracting the characteristic wave. Next, we build the analyzer from the training data using multiple discriminant analysis. The analyzer is able to determine the input data belongs to which the groups (up, down, right, left). In the running process, the input data is an observation EOG data for controlling something like machine, PC, etc, and is categorized the groups (up, down, right, left) by the classifier which is created based on the analyzer. In other words, the classifier decides the eye direction.

3.3   The Simulation Test

In the simulation test, we created the core function of monitoring system based on our algorithm and simulated behavior on monitoring eye movement. The participants were 2 males and were investigated EOG data accompanying eye moment as the training and input data like the pre-experiment (however, the direction is 4: up, down, right, left) by the Emotiv headset. The examples of training data and input data are shown in Figure 7. Figure 8 shows the results of the training data and the input data groups classified by the analyzer and classifier in the simulation test. In this test, the results of our classifier for the raining data and the input data were an average accuracy of about 99% and about 89% in the modified case.

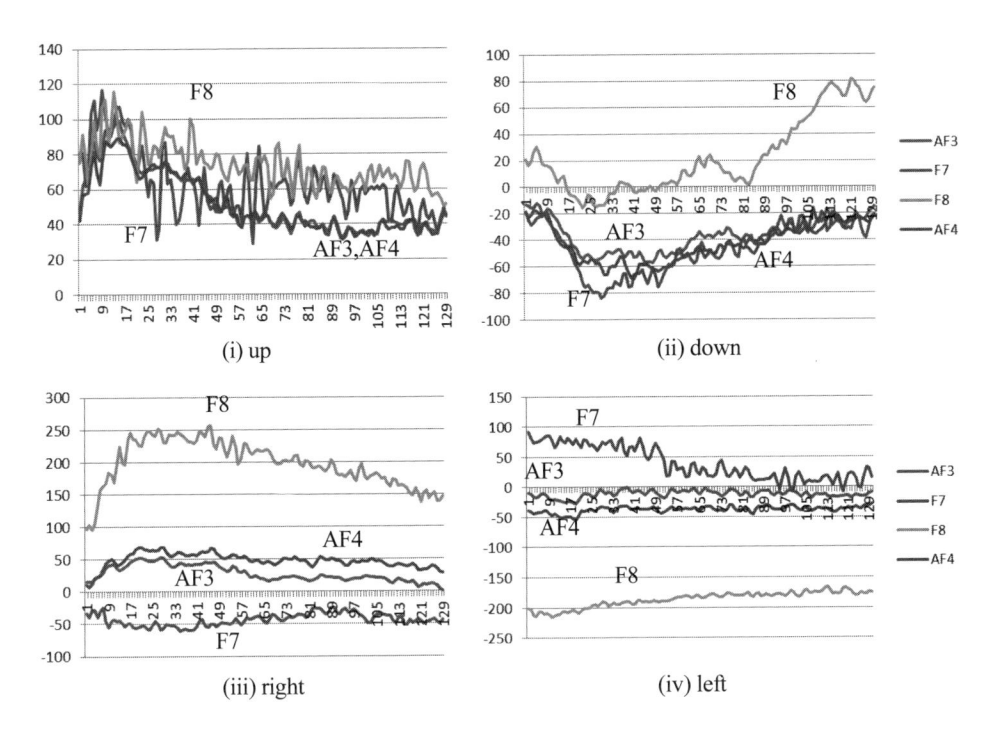

(i) up   (ii) down

(iii) right   (iv) left

(a) Training data

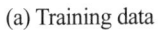
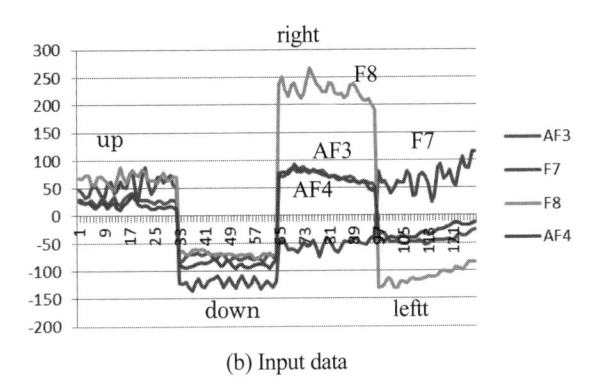

(b) Input data

Figure 7. Examples of training data and input data

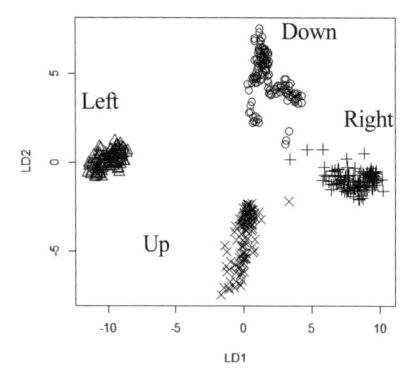

	Down	Left	Right	Up
Down	130	0	0	0
Left	0	130	0	0
Right	3	0	127	0
Up	0	0	0	130

(a) Training data

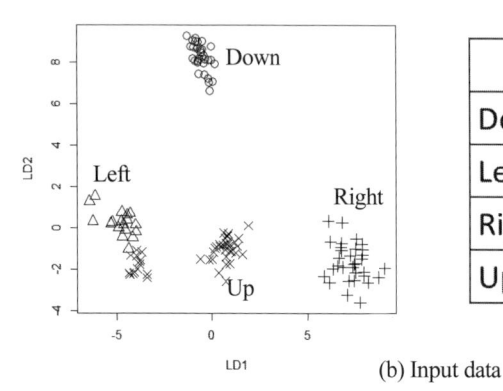

	Down	Left	Right	Up
Down	32	0	0	0
Left	0	18	0	14
Right	0	0	32	0
Up	0	0	0	32

(b) Input data

Figure 8.   Results of classifying training data and input data

4. Conclusion

In this paper, we have developed an algorithm for monitoring eye movement using wireless electroencephalogram (EEG) headset such as Emotiv Epoc Premium (Emotiv headset). Our method is able to adapt to devices of human interfaces, Brain Machine Interface (BCI), Brain Computer Interface (BCI), etc. In the simulation tests, the results show that our algorithm can discriminate among the eye movement with an average accuracy of about 90% in the simplified case.

In the future plan, we'll analyze eye blink and fixation for the trigger act clicking an icon by a mouse cursor and develop software for applying our algorithm to connecting the Emotiv EGG headset.

Acknowledgements

This research is supported by the 2013 and the 2014 grants of Hiroshima International University.

References

[1] Paulo Vinicius Koerich Borges, Nicola Conci, Andrea Cavallaro, "Video-Based Human Behavior Understanding: A Survey", IEEE Transactions on Circuits and Systems for Video Technology, 23, 11, pp.1993-2008 (2013).

[2] Henry Y.T. Ngan, Hideki Kawai, Kazuo Kunieda, Keiji Yamada, "Social Behavior Analysis in Visual Human Monitoring System: A Survey and Perspective", *Social and Information Networks* (2016).

[3] Avtansh Singh, Vandana Vikas Thakare, "Applications Of Sensors To Detect The Behavior Of Human. A Survey Paper", IRJET, 4, 7, pp.404-406 (2017).

[4] Hiroki TAMURA, Mingmin YAN, Masaki MIYASHITA, Takao MANABE, Koichi TANNO and Yasufumi FUSE, "Development of Mouse Cursor Control System using DC and AC Elements of Electrooculogram Signals and its Applications", *IC-MED Journal*, Vol.5, No.1, pp3-15 (2013).

[5] B. Šumak, Matic Špindler, M. Pušnik, "Design and development of contactless interaction with computers based on the Emotiv EPOC+ device", MIPRO, pp.576-581 (2017).

[6] Ha Hoang Kha, Vo Anh Kha, Dinh Quoc Hung, "Brainwave-controlled applications with the Emotiv EPOC using support vector machine", ICITACEE, pp.106-111 (2016).

[7] Daniel P. Prince, Mark J. Edmonds, Andrew J. Sutter, Matthew Thomas Cusumano, Wenjie Lu, Vijayan K. Asari, "Brain machine interface using Emotiv EPOC to control robai cyton robotic arm", NAECON, pp.263-266 (2015).

[8] Yasui Y, "A brainwave signal measurement and data processing technique for daily life applications", *J Physiol Anthropol*, 28(3), pp.145-50 (2009).

[9] Laura Kauhanen, Pasi Jylänki, Janne Lehtonen, Pekka Rantanen, Hannu Alaranta, Mikko Sams, "EEG-Based Brain-Computer Interface for Tetraplegics", Comput Intell Neurosci, (2007).

[10] Emotiv - Brain Computer Interface Technology, from http://www.emotiv.com

[11] Fisher, R. A., "The use of multiple measurements in taxonomic problems", *Annual Eugenic*, Vol.7, No.2, pp179-188 (1936).

Chapter 3

Big Data Techniques for Measuring Global Flow of Funds[*]

Nan Zhang

Faculty of Economic Sciences, Hiroshima Shudo University

1-1 Ozuka-Higashi 1-chome, Asaminami-ku, Hiroshima, 731-3159 Japan

Abstract

Big data refers to the conventional software tools in a certain period to crawl the content management and the data set. Big Data Technology (BDT) refers to the various types of data, the ability to quickly obtain valuable information. It is suitable for big data technology, including database, data mining, distributed file system, distributed database, cloud computing platform, the Internet, and scalable storage system. BDT can also be used to compile monetary and financial statistics, especially to measure the Global Flow of Funds (GFF). This paper is focuses on building a statistical framework for measuring GFF, explore how to use BDT to integrates the data sources, and improve the timeliness of the existing data transmission. Applying BDT to measure GFF can provide important basis for policy authorities to guard against financial risks.

Keywords: Global Flow of Funds, Statistical Framework, Data Sources, Big Data, Data Gap

1. Introduction

Global Flow of Funds (GFF) is an extension of the domestic flow of funds. It connects domestic economies with the rest of the world. GFF data could provide valuable information for analyzing interconnectedness across borders, global liquidity flows, and global financial

[*] This research was supported by the grants-in-aid for scientific research (Scientific Research（C）, 16KT0185).

interdependencies. Corresponding to a sharp change in the financial market, a few researchers began looking at the GFF beginning in the 1990s. Ishida (1993) put forward the idea of GFF analysis, discussed the concept of GFF, and measured the international capital flows between Japan, the U.S., and Germany. He extended the scope of flow-of-funds analysis from the national to global level and suggested international capital flows should be included in the GFF.

In April 2009, the G20 Finance Ministers and Central Bank Governors Working Group on Reinforcing International Co-Operation and Promoting Integrity in Financial Markets called on the International Monetary Fund (IMF) and the Financial Stability Board (FSB) to identify information gaps and provide appropriate proposals for strengthening data collection and reporting back to the Finance Ministers and Central Bank Governors. As a result of this meeting, the IMF and FSB proposed maintenance and expansion of the existing statistics in October 2009. The principal focus was Recommendation 15, as financial and economic crises are characterized by abrupt revaluations or other changes in the capital positions of key sectors of the economy. Recommendation 15 states that, "the IAG, which includes all agencies represented in the Inter-Secretariat Working Group on National Accounts, to develop a strategy to promote the compilation and dissemination of the Balance Sheet Approach (BSA), Flow of Funds, and sectoral data more generally, starting with the G-20 economies. Data on nonbank financial institutions should be a particular priority," etc.[1] Thus, Recommendation 15 also implies, through its reference to compiling "flow of funds" statistics, the compilation of breakdowns of financial positions and flows of each economic sector by its counterparty sectors. Datasets providing this kind of information are said to provide "from-whom-to-whom (W-to-W)" financial statistics. In such a situation, we also need to understand and measure the flow of funds between countries, namely the Global Flow of Funds (GFF).

Shrestha, Mink and Fassler (2012) described the importance of using an integrated approach for the compilation of financial flows and positions on a from-whom-to-whom (W-to-W) basis, one of the main components of Recommendation 15 of the G20 Data Gaps Initiative. The global financial crisis of 2008 highlighted the need to understand financial interconnectedness among the various sectors of an economy and their counterparties in the rest of the world. However, the application of this kind of analysis has been hampered due to inadequate data. This paper discusses the development of statistical methodologies and data availability, supporting the compilation of partial data on a W-to-W basis.

Stone (1966) set up the balance sheets of a closed economy in a standard matrix form, distinguishing between financial assets and real assets on the assets side and between liabilities to third parties and liabilities to self on the liabilities side. In Stone's (1966) matrix, the first n row and column pairs relate to sectors; each row contains a sector's assets, and the corresponding column contains its liabilities. The following m row and column pairs relate to financial claims; each row contains the holdings of a particular claim as a liability, and the corresponding column contains the holdings of the same claim as an asset. The penultimate row

---

[1] Financial Stability Board and International Monetary Fund (2009). The Financial Crisis and Information Gaps—Report to the G-20 Finance Ministers and Central Bank Governors, p.10.

and column pair relate to the real assets and accumulated saving in the various sectors, and the final row and column pair simply relate to totals. This paper considers that it was also a matrix based on the W-to-W format.

On the other hand, there is international awareness of the issue that existing statistical data do not describe the risks inherent in a financial system. Previous research has evolved into a discussion of the basic concept of GFF and a proposal to establish a statistical framework for GFF (Zhang, 2005; Tujimua, 2008). The recent global crisis showed how easily shocks in one country are transmitted and amplified as well as how liquidity in financial markets spread quickly across national borders. Therefore, the IMF's Statistics Department has already organized seven economies with systemically important financial centers to construct a GFF mapping domestic and external capital stocks, with a geographical break down (Luca et al., 2013). The main purpose of Luca et al. is to conceptually map the financial interlinkages reflected in the Balance of Payments (BOP) and the International Investment Position (IIP) statistics and in the "rest-of-the-world" (ROW) account of national accounts. The paper sets out the concepts and existing data sources. The Balance Sheet Approach is used to break down the rest of the world by IIP components. An external statistics' matrix (metadata) exercise shows what external-sector financial data are available by using IIP concept. The main outcome is a prototype template of stock and flow data, geographically broken down by national/regional economies.

Another working paper on GFF was published by Luca et al. in 2014, which presents an approach to understanding the U.S. shadow banking system using a new GFF conceptual framework developed by the IMF's Statistics Department. The GFF uses external stock and flow matrices to map claims between sector–location pairs. Their findings highlight the large positions and gross flows of the U.S. banking sector (ODCs) and its interconnectedness with banking sectors in the Euro area and United Kingdom. European counterparties are large holders of U.S. other financial corporations (OFCs) debt securities. Luca et al. (2014) also explore the relationship between credit to domestic entities and the growth of non-core liabilities.

This means that observation of GFF has not remained mere theoretical research, but has entered the stage of experiment and statistical application. In order to measure financial stress and observe the spillover effect of systematic financial crises through GFF and to observe the situation triggering an international financial crisis, research on creation and analysis of GFF statistics is further needed.

Zhang (2016)'s paper reviewed the definition of GFF, clarified the integrated framework for measuring GFF, and attempted to carry out the compilation of the GFFS for external financial positions and flows on a from-whom-to-whom basis. In addition, it will potentially fill some important data gaps in currently available macroeconomic statistics. The paper elaborated on the main attributes of the integrated macroeconomic accounts and the GFF matrix, which allows it to serve as the framework for compiling sector accounts, including financial positions and flows on a from-whom-to-whom basis.

However, for GFF statistics creation, integration of data sources and timely collection of data are very important issues. This paper referenced "the report of the Financial Crisis and Information Gaps" that was prepared by the FSB and the IMF (2009) and BDT. The main purpose of the paper is to measure GFF and apply the result to regular monitoring of the GFF. The composition of this paper is as follows. Firstly, according to the concept of GFF (Zhang, 2005), this paper will make an integrated framework for measuring GFF. Secondly, data sources and approach, is also very important. The paper sets out the concepts and existing data sources, and the BSA is used to break down the rest of the world by components of IMF data sources and BIS data sources. The third part, the paper will discuss how to use big data technology to resolve the integration of data sources, and to collect data timely for measuring GFF. The main outcomes and the issues which remain are summarized within the conclusion.

2. Statistical Framework of Global Flow of Funds

In order to measure financial stress and observe the spread effect of systematic financial crises through GFF, a new statistical framework is needed that corresponds to the operational structure of GFF. Especially, an integrated framework should be used as the foundation of a statistical monitoring system. When the flow of funds in financial markets is tied up with the balance of payments, the rest of the world sector will have an excess of outflowing funds (net capital outflows) if the current account is in surplus. Conversely, the domestic sector will have an excess of inflowing funds. Therefore, when the real economic side of the domestic and overseas economy is analyzed under an open economic system, the balance of savings-investment in the domestic economy corresponds to the current account balance. However, the outflow of domestic net funds corresponds to the capital account balance when we examine the financial relationship between domestic and external flows of funds. For this reason, relationships among the domestic savings-investment balance, financial surplus or deficit, current account, and external flow of funds should be expressed in an integrated framework to enable joint routine monitoring of GFF.

Table 1 is in accordance with IIP statistical standards and is based on a structure wherein the from-whom-to-whom data are used to establish the GFF statistical framework, and is keeping the double-entry principle. According to the statistical standards of IIP, which are based on Balance of Payments and sixth edition of the International Investment Position Manual (BPM6), the IIP can be set as the foreign financial assets and external debt. Each column corresponds to the balance sheet of a country in question, with country, assets, and liabilities then listed in rows by instrument with the counterparty country identified for each cell.

Table 1 provides a statistical framework for deriving the GFF matrix. Assets are subdivided into five parts: direct investment, portfolio investment, financial derivatives, other investments, and reserve assets; the liabilities are divided into four parts: direct investment, portfolio investment, financial derivatives, and other investments. The net financial position is external financial assets plus reserve assets minus liabilities. By this statistical framework, the GFF statistics can reflect stock information of financial assets and liabilities between the world and a region at a particular time. However, the GFF statistics remain consistent with IIP Statistics Standard, and also have its unique statistics establishment method, which can be summarized as follows:

Table 1. Global Flow of Funds Matrix for a Country

Issuer of liability (debtor) \\ Holder of liability (creditor)	Financial Instruments	a Rest of the World	b Country A	c Country B	d ...	e All Other Economies	f Total Liabilities of Financial Instruments	g Total Liabities	
Rest of the World	Direct investment								1
	Portfolio investment								2
	Financial derivatives								3
	Other investment								4
Country A	Direct investment								5
	Portfolio investment								6
	Financial derivatives								7
	Other investment								8
Country B	Direct investment								9
	Portfolio investment								10
	Financial derivatives								11
	Other investment								12
......	......								13
All other economies	Direct investment								14
	Portfolio investment								15
	Financial derivatives								16
	Other investment								17
Total Asset of Financial Instruments	Direct investment								18
	Portfolio investment								19
	Financial derivatives								20
	Other investment								21
Total Asset									22
Net Worth									23
Reserve assets									24
Monetary gold									25
Special drawing rights									26
Reserve position in the fund									27
Other reserve assets									28
Net error and omission									29
Net Financial Position									30

(1) In order to reflect the relationship between W-to-W, GFF statistics use the parallel processing method wherein transaction and countries (sectors) are rows, namely, by putting the transaction items that direct investments, securities investments, financial derivatives, and other investments to countries (sectors) in the rows, whereas each country (sector) is in the columns.

Accordingly, we can determine the dual relationship of a transaction item in countries (sectors), which can show the scale of the transaction item and reflect from-whom-to-whom-by-what relationships in a two-way format. For example, a5–a8 in the table show the rest of world transactions in a country in the columns by showing which financial instruments are used for transactions bringing how much funds to country A that in the row. As this can provide two-way information about the financing structure of rest of world in a country with country A, we also can know the financing scale and corresponding information on counterparties. At the same time, we can also get the information of where country A is located in the row vectors from other countries to raise funds and total amount. We can also get relevant information on country B in the row vectors on its fundraising from the rest of the world, country A, etc.

(2) To reflect the actual situation of international capital in a country or a region, and in order to establish the GFF matrix table for the application analysis, we set countries (sectors) in rows and columns by the principle of W-to-W tabulating. We also designed an "All Other economies" sector (see the column e and row 9–12 that can be represented as e9, e10, e11, e12). The relationship of these "All Other economies" and the world total can be expressed as the follows: "Liabilities of All Other economies" = Total Liabilities – Liabilities of the total for specific countries. That is, e9=f9-(a9+b9+c9+d9), … , e12=f12-(a12+b12+c12+d12).

(3) Each "column" shows a country how to use funds by transaction item, namely, who outputs how much funds by what item; each "row" represent how a country raises funds through four financial instruments, namely, who inputs how much funds by what item. The difference between the total of the row and column in row 23, which shows the balance between use of external funds financing for a certain country at a particular point in time, that is, the net output of funds. For instance, Country A's net worth equals country A's total asset minus its total liabilities, that is, b23=b22-(g5+g6+g7+g8).

(4) Corresponding to the various transaction instruments of various countries, rows 24–28 show part of the reserve assets, specifically monetary gold, special drawing rights, reserve positions in the fund, and other reserve assets. Put reserve assets as an instrument in Table 1 is to show a balance relationship between net worth and net financial position, and also is can show its components. For example, country A's component of reserve assets, can show as b24=b25+b26+b27+b28.

(5) The bottom row in Table 1, namely row 30, reflects net international investment position. The data are gathered from IIP, in order to reflect overall equilibrium conditions of external financial position in a country, need to set the Net error and omission in row 29. Net financial position of each country is calculating using net worth that also can call as net financial investment plus the total reserve assets and the net error and omission, such as a30 = a23+ a24 + a29, …, e30 = e23 + e24 + e30.

(6)   Because the main purpose of preparing the GFF matrix table is to observe the cross-border capital positions and flows, so the diagonal line elements in GFF matrix are zero, namely, each transaction is a domestic to a foreign country and does not include a country's internal financial investments. In fact, as the data sources (CDIS, CPIS, and CBS) are also in

accordance with observation of cross-border capital positions to the statistical classification, these data sources can fulfill the conditions that each diagonal line elements in the GFF matrix needs to become zero.

3. Data Sources for Measuring Global Flow of Funds

The GFF metadata should be based on existing statistical data and therefore share many similarities of approach with them. The GFF data sources include not only the "rest-of-the-world" account of national accounts, but also monetary and financial statistics, IIP statistics, and BIS international banking statistics. The prototype template for the main data is shown in Figure 1. There are two metadata sources for measuring GFF: (1) data sources for making the DAL matrix, and (2) data sources for establishing the EAL matrix. These two matrices thus cover the DAL and the EAL, and they could be extended to flow data. We will discuss the two data sources, which summarize the concepts, draw out what data are available, and identify the major data gaps.

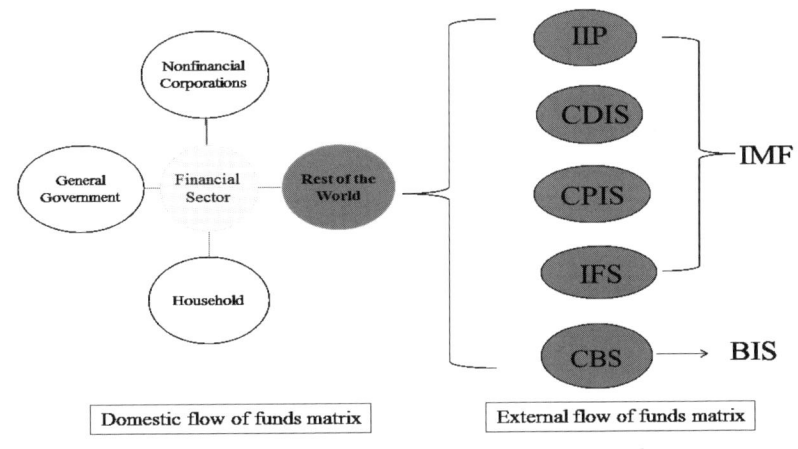

Figure 1. Prototype template for measuring GFF

The DAL matrix is based on the Balance Sheet Approach (BSA), with the rest of world sector data drawn from the national accounts and IIP. The EAL matrix presents metadata on whatever external sector financial stock data are available by IIP category, drawing on IMF and BIS data sources. The IIP is the link between domestic and external matrices. This paper will focus on the EAL data sources and integrate with the economic variables to establish the GFF matrix.

Data from IMF's Monetary and Financial Statistics, IIP, and the national accounts are used to derive the BSA matrix. The BSA matrix can provide information about a country's or region's financial corporations' stock positions for residents and nonresidents. In the EAL matrix, the datasets with bilateral counterpart country details are collected by the IMF and BIS as Table 2

(1) Foreign direct investment: The Coordinated Direct Investment Survey (CDIS) provides

bilateral counterpart country details on "inward" direct investment positions (i.e., direct investment into the reporting economy) cross-classified by the economy of immediate investors. It also provides data on "outward" direct investment positions (i.e., direct investment abroad by the reporting economy), cross-classified by the economy of immediate investment, as well as mirror data for all economies. The CDIS database contains breakdowns of direct investment position data, including, in most instances, separate data on net equity and net debt positions, as well as tables that present "mirror" data[2].

(2) Portfolio investment: The Coordinated Portfolio Investment Survey (CPIS) provides bilateral counterpart country details covering holdings of asset stock positions by reporting economies and derived liabilities for all economies. The CPIS's purpose is to improve statistics on holdings of portfolio investment assets in the form of equity, long-term debt, and short-term debt. It is also used to collect comprehensive information, including geographical detail on the issuer's country of residence, stock of cross-border equities, long-term bonds and notes, and short-term debt instruments, for use in the compilation or improvement of IIP statistics on portfolio investment capital.

Table 2. Datasets for Measuring Global Flow of Funds

Items	Data source	Frequency	Geographic coverage	Letest update	Temporal coverage	Benchmark	Web address
Direct Investment	CDIS (IIP)	Annual	106 reporters on Inwart 71 reporters on Outward Cross-classified	12/12/2016	beginning end-2009	BPM6	http://cdis.imf.org
Portfolio Investment	CPIS (IIP)	Annual	86 reporters	03/23/2017	beginning end-2001	BPM6	http://data.imf.org/
		Semi-annua	72 reporters		beginning end-june 2013		
			Cross-classified				
Financial Derivative	CPIS	Annual & Quarterly		03/31/2017	beginning end-june 2013	BPM6	http://data.imf.org/
	IIP	Annual & Quarterly		05/24/2017			
Other Investment	LBS by BIS	Quarterly	46 reporters by locational basis	04/20/2017	Q1.1999-Q4.2016	SNA, BPM6	http://stats.bis.org/stat
	CBS by BIS	Quarterly	31 reporters by ultimate risk basis	04/20/2017	Q2.1998-Q4.2016		http://stats.bis.org/stat
	IIP	Annual & Quarterly					
Reserve Assets	IFS	Annual, Quarterly Monthly	194 reporters	05/24/2017	beginnng 1948	SNA, MFS, BPM6	http://data.imf.org/
	COFER	Quarterly	146 reporters	03/31/2017	beginning 1999	BPM6	http://data.imf.org/
	IIP	Annual	152 reporters	05/24/2017	from 1945 onward	BPM6	http://data.imf.org/
		Quarterly	152 reporters		from 2009 onward		

Notes: IMF, **http://data.imf.org/?sk=388DFA60-1D26-4ADE-B505-A05A558D9A42&sId=1469115547122**

BIS, http://stats.bis.org/statx/toc/LBS.html; http://stats.bis.org/statx/toc/CBS.html, June 1, 2017.

(3) Other investment: Other investment is a residual category that includes positions and transactions other than those included in direct investment, portfolio investment, financial

---

[2] The term "mirror" data refers to the tables in which data from the reporting economy are shown side-by-side with the data obtained from all other counterpart reporting economies.

derivatives and employee stock options, and reserve assets[3]. Other investment includes (a) other equity; (b) currency and deposits; (c) loans (including use of IMF credit and IMF loans); (d) nonlife insurance technical reserves, life insurance and annuity entitlements, pension entitlements, and provisions for calls under standardized guarantees; (e) trade credit and advances; (f) other accounts receivable/payable; and (g) SDR allocations (SDR holdings are included in reserve assets). In order to reflect the bilateral counterpart country for loans, deposits, and other assets and liabilities, this paper uses the related dataset with BIS International Banking Statistics (IBS) instead of IIP Statistics.

(4) The BIS compiles and publishes two sets of statistics on international banking activity, namely the Locational Banking Statistics (LBS) and Consolidated Banking Statistics (CBS). LBS provide information about the currency composition of banks' balance sheets and the geographical breakdown of their counterparties. They capture outstanding claims and liabilities of banks located in 46 reporting countries[4], including intragroup positions between offices of the same banking group. The locational statistics are compiled following principles that are consistent with balance of payments. CBS measure banks' country risk exposures. They capture the worldwide consolidated claims of internationally active banks headquartered in BIS reporting countries which include 31 countries. The consolidated statistics include the claims of banks' foreign affiliates but exclude intragroup positions, similarly to the consolidation approach followed by banking supervisors. They detail the transfer of credit risk from the immediate counterparty to the country of ultimate risk (where the guarantor of a claim resides). This paper utilizes CBS[5] in the dataset because it measures banks' country risk exposures. The CBS data capture the worldwide consolidated claims of internationally active banks headquartered in BIS-reporting countries. The consolidated statistics include claims of banks' foreign affiliates but exclude intragroup positions, similar to the consolidation approach followed by banking supervisors. They detail the transfer of credit risk from the immediate counterparty to the country of ultimate risk (where the claim guarantor resides). In addition, CBS data provide quarterly information on claims and liabilities of banks vis-à-vis banks and nonbanks in other countries worldwide based on the country of ultimate risk or residence of the creditor bank and can also be used to mirror data for non-reporting countries. The CBS data can be used in the external statistics' matrix.

(5) For data on reserve assets, we obtained the data template from the IIP, and the Currency Composition of Official Foreign Exchange Reserves (COFER) provide country-level data, while the Survey of Securities Held as Foreign Exchange Reserves (SEFER) provides

---

[3] IMF, *Balance of Payments Manual,* 6th edition (BPM6), 111, 2014.

[4] Countries reporting the international banking statistics are shown by http://www.bis.org/statistics/rep_countries.htm

[5] A BIS-organized data collection that measures banks' country risk exposures. It captures the worldwide consolidated positions of banks headquartered in BIS reporting countries, including positions of their foreign affiliates but excluding intragroup positions. Central banks or other national authorities collect data from internationally active banks headquartered in their jurisdiction, compile national aggregate data, and then report these to the BIS to calculate global aggregates.

counterpart country data for all SEFER reporters as a group. To supplement data on reserve assets, International Financial Statistics (IFS), which includes World Total Reserves, World Gold, World Reserve Position in the Fund, World SDR Holdings, and World Foreign Exchange, can also be used.

But no matter what kind of reserves assets data are not counterparty information, it cannot constitute a matrix form, and neither can it reflect the relationship between countries based on W-to-W form. Therefore, in order to observe the balance of a country's external assets and overall liabilities; as a reference, IIP data alone can be used to fill the cell on reserve assets.

In order to observe the overall net position, in this paper, IIP data have been used to supplement the data for constructing the EAL matrix. The IIP is a subset of a national balance sheet, the net IIP plus the value of nonfinancial assets equaling the net worth of the economy, which is the balancing item of the national balance sheet. The IIP relates to a point in time, usually at the beginning (opening value) or the end (closing value) of the period.

GFFS can provide a statistical framework if concepts, definitions, and classifications underlying these statistics are standardized across economies. Fortunately, these standards can be obtained from 2008SNA, the IMF's Monetary and financial statistics manual and compilation guide (2016) and Balance of Payments Manual (BPM6), and the BIS's Guidelines for Reporting the BIS International Banking Statistics. Based on the statistical framework and data sources described above, we tried to compile the GFF statistics matrix, as shown in Table 3. Confined to the length of the paper, we omit the description of Table 3, which will discuss it in other paper.

4.   Big Data in Global Flow of Funds

When we read Table 3, we can know that it is not easy to compile this table. It needs to use many different data sources with different statistical criteria, and some of which had a long lag time. Through the above research of constructing statistical framework and arranging data sources, we can conclude that the key problem for establishing GFF statistics is the benchmark of data sources and timeliness of data reporting. Some data that are compiled by IMF and BIS which both based on the BPM6, but some parts of the data are overlapping. For example, CPIS is compiled by IMF, which mainly consists of securities statistics, while banking statistics are made by BIS, but banking credit business also include some securities trading. That is, data collected from different sources have some overlapping and omitted. If we can make a same benchmark for data sources, it will facilitate in data collection and improve the quality of data. If we improve the timeliness of reporting data, it will be easy to data compilation, thereby ensure the timeliness of data publication.

4.1   Way Need to Use Big Data Technology for Measuring GFF

Therefore, we need to solve two issues for establishing GFF. One is to clear benchmarks on data source; and another is to use Big Data techniques to solve the standardization of data transmission, reduce statistical errors, and improve the timeliness of data publication to reflect the changes of financial risk. As shown in Table 2, the lag of the data published by CDIS is more than one year, and the lag period of CPIS publication is 6 months, which cannot meet the needs of financial regulation. In the following sections, we will focus on applying big data technologies to solve the standardization of data transmission and to improve data timeliness.

Big data is a term for data sets that are so large or complex that traditional data processing application software is inadequate to deal with them. Challenges include capture, storage, analysis, data curation, search, sharing, transfer, visualization, querying, and updating and information privacy. Big data can be described by the following five basic characteristics.

The first is Volume. The quantity of generated and stored data. The size of the data determines the value and potential insight- and whether it can actually be considered big data or not. The second is Variety. The type and nature of the data. This helps people who analyze it to effectively use the resulting insight. The third is Velocity. In this context, the speed at which the data is generated and processed to meet the demands and challenges that lie in the path of growth and development. The fourth is Variability. Inconsistency of the data set can hamper processes to handle and manage it. The fifth is Veracity. The quality of captured data can vary greatly, affecting accurate analysis.

Through the above general interpretation on big data, we can know that the preparation of GFF data as well as the monetary and financial statistics also have the characteristics of big data, big data technology can be used to handle GFF data and application analysis.

We think that it can be put forward by the international institutions, such as the IMF, to put forward a proposal to the member of countries for establishing a network data transfer agreement concerning the submission of direct investment, securities investment, financial derivative products, and international banking. In this way, some international institutions can popularize the standardization of data transmission, and it can improve the timeliness of data transmission. Through the timely monitoring of GFF, we can track massive behavioral data on international capital flows from the Internet, mining analysis, reveal the regularity of GFF, and put forward the research conclusion and countermeasures.

4.2   How to Use Big Data Technology for Measuring GFF

In the big data era of financial, a large number of financial products and trading to show through the network, including fixed network and mobile network. Among them, the mobile network will gradually become a major channel of big data financial transactions. With the law and the regulatory policy are improved, and the continuous development of big data technology, there will be more and more rich the financial products and transactions, and gathering financial information through the network is also becoming more and more convenient.

4.2.1   Integrate the data sources of CDIS, CPIS and IIP

Application of BDT in finance field including GFF, which have three levels. The first is to integrate the internet data source, the second is to make the common statistical standard of

Table 3. Example GFF Matrix (millions of US dollars, End-December 2015)

Issuer of liability (debtor) / Holder of claim (creditor)	Financial Instruments	Canada	China	France	Germany	Italy	Japan	Korea	Netherlands	Switzerland	United Kingdom	United States	All Other Economies	Total of Financial Instruments	Total Liabilities
Canada	Direct investment		14871	5705	9749	1155	15896	2329	64350	8857	24759	280124	127457	555251	2868691
	Portfolio investment		3710	18658	38808	3676	55607	3294	18489	34680	37483	703300	306614	1224319	
	Financial derivatives														
	Other investment		11281	20239	24742	1200	34277	2330	12307	3910	104664	833856	40315	1089121	
China	Direct investment	11313		23292	66637	7430	151926	61239	31459	12142	18912	78490	2116724	2579564	4299674
	Portfolio investment	19396		10317	5265	418	16630	13955	11795	5417	47982	113816	531419	776410	
	Financial derivatives														
	Other investment	79959		141343	123646	36008	40545	6457	52540	80254	139802	139157	103988	943700	
France	Direct investment	3391	2022		63414	15126	15802	1077	80190	76958	71696	71504	258925	660107	5501960
	Portfolio investment	35265	4906		359091	141637	222314	10593	187006	82509	302137	469625	1101541	2916625	
	Financial derivatives														
	Other investment	27403	37845		148282	278091	150090	13980	94151	66414	233868	434245	440859	1925228	
Germany	Direct investment	1737	1963	45145		36931	20946	4961	151506	52333	68035	78123	325262	786941	5271823
	Portfolio investment	29426	4999	231018		74816	128649	5155	225401	82766	288405	378630	1351440	2800704	
	Financial derivatives														
	Other investment	29232	26464	169935		91573	34615	11617	114185	70935	358785	433362	343475	1684178	
Italy	Direct investment	334	107	59058	23765		3009	399	68319	17731	39444	7565	117352	337083	2123958
	Portfolio investment	6990	1164	263595	183564		53713	1159	45932	9945	131576	106171	492602	1296410	
	Financial derivatives														
	Other investment	2472	2924	39867	178185		6253	120	17984	12394	41511	36403	152352	490465	
Japan	Direct investment	1160	655	24865	2332	930		3190	24719	8966	13173	51573	39136	170698	4523993
	Portfolio investment	53301	10691	109160	27305	5147		11665	41081	26431	213004	806703	547489	1851976	
	Financial derivatives														
	Other investment	61351	70127	153031	98373	29588		47952	84598	26539	188349	1414069	327341	2501318	
Korea	Direct investment	1500	4669	5315	6921	198	44767		15428	3492	13112	33034	41222	169659	685145
	Portfolio investment	13865	3251	7350	8296	776	25196		10491	10864	37311	171011	139122	427533	
	Financial derivatives														
	Other investment	2411	21656	1065	3051	573	9706		865	1546	4046	25431	17603	87953	
Netherlands	Direct investment	8406	22460	131413	170863	88976	50684	2628		256832	364574	790385	2052195	3939415	6546057
	Portfolio investment	16909	2647	259375	228784	47253	118160	4055		70714	177752	412984	552359	1890991	
	Financial derivatives														
	Other investment	14625		73721	150700	28230	10542			24716	97160	172686	143271	715651	
Switzerland	Direct investment	-311		40662	25506	4374	5765		183523		38968	93969	470170	862624	2856086
	Portfolio investment	25486	4105	27053	47986	9867	28919	4320	23601		85498	431068	212426	900329	
	Financial derivatives														
	Other investment	20890	15749	70221	69085	20603	20283	7239	32133		218338	514360	104232	1093133	
United Kingdom	Direct investment	34399	2707	109080	82782	9520	67729	3614	231565	61917		432987	518003	1554303	6807677
	Portfolio investment	77623	12452	239845	198978	67767	171104	16509	114334	78949		1244554	1127021	3349136	
	Financial derivatives														
	Other investment	83674	151375	146114	143197	31916	98754	59704	93539	52227		740268	303470	1904238	
United States	Direct investment	268972	14838	233844	255471	28648	411201	40130	282525	257859	483841		856870	3134199	15265593
	Portfolio investment	748521	111144	245894	320482	84124	1369423	98555	425217	272133	968186		5592270	10235949	
	Financial derivatives														
	Other investment	102148	86309	153752	157067	50224	284545	71222	79299	54901	414491		441487	1895445	
All other economies	Direct investment	307177	452526	381373	423680	113543	374340	51444	1729565	357084	1089795	2140655		13655760	34571254
	Portfolio investment	188559	121761	1117771	1487060	774606	1321977	66613	606882	558235	1489395	4609854		18555376	
	Financial derivatives														
	Other investment	22283	297870	111441	117499	67564	55210	9654	73136	34837	764622	588178		2360118	
Total Asset of Financial Instruments	Direct investment	638078	516818	1059751	1131120	306831	1162065	171011	2863149	1114170	2226308	4058409	13157896	28405605	91321910
	Portfolio investment	1215340	280830	2530037	2905617	1210087	3511692	235872	1710229	1232641	3778730	9447716	18166966	46225757	
	Financial derivatives														
	Other investment	446448	721600	1080729	1213827	635570	744820	230275	654737	428673	2565636	5332015	2636217	16690548	
Total Asset		2299866	1519248	4670517	5250564	2152488	5418577	637158	5228115	2775483	8570674	18838140	33961079	91321910	
Net Worth		-568824	-2780426	-831443	-21259	28530	894585	-47987	-1317942	-80603	1762998	3572547	-610174		
Reserve assets		79753	3406112	138163	173684	130770	1232756	367944	38260	606109	129536	383601			
Monetary gold		58	60191	82963	115176	83736	26116	4795	20917	35749	10593	277189			
Special drawing rights		7899	10284	13058	16533	8307	18047	3239	6535	4716	13238	49688			
Reserve position in the fund		2719	4547	4113	5588	3014	9471	1397	1970	1611	4197	17609			
Other reserve assets		69077	3331089	38020	36387	35714	1179122	358514	8836	564032	101509	39115			
Net erroe and omisions		839496	970767	278953	1461025	-589991	688062	-124695	1727524	88025	-2291506	-11236785			
Net Financial Position		350425	1596453	-414327	1613450	-430691	2815402	195262	447841	613531	-398972	-7280637			

Data Source: IMF, Coordinated Direct Investment Survey (CDIS), Coordinated Portfolio Investment Survey (CPIS), http://www.imf.org/external/data.htm, and International Investment Position Statistics (BOP/IIP) http://data.imf.org/?sk=7A51304B-6426-40C0-83DD-CA473CA1FD52 on 4/17/2017;

BIS international banking statistics, http://www.bis.org/statistics/consstats.htm on 4/20/2017.

different data sources, and the third is to establish the subject classification and coding standard system. As noted above, the data source of GFF is mainly from IMF and BIS. IMF data source can be divided into CDIS, CPIS, IIP, but the statistical methods of CDIS and CPIS are different with IIP. CDIS and CPIS are the same stock data, including cross-border matrix, which can reflect the situation of counterparties. IIP is the stock data too, provides the data about of direct investment, securities investment, financial derivatives, other investment, and reserve assets. However, IIP's data only reflects each countries' respective external financial positions, and does not include the information of counterparties. Therefore, we need to integrate the data source of CDIS, CPIS and IIP, that make an instrument of a country in IIP consistent with CDIS and CPIS. For instance, make that the total assets of direct investment of Country A in table 1 is equal to the assets of direct investment of the same country in IIP, and the total liabilities of direct investment of Country A in table 1 is equal to the liabilities of direct investment of the same country in IIP. This can ensures that IIP is in the same statistical range with CDIS and CPIS, and it can avoid double calculations and omissions.

4.2.2 Consistency of statistical standards: Treatment of Other Investments

In the third section of this paper, as a conceptual introduction, we explain concept of other investment instrument and its data souse. Other investment covers other equity; currency and deposits; loans; insurance, pension and standardized guarantee schemes; trade credit and advances; other accounts receivable/payable-other; and special drawing rights (SDRs) [6]. However, other investment has not compiled as a matrix form, as CDIS or CPIS. Therefore, as an alternative method and data acquisition possibility, we adopt the data of CBS, which belongs to the BIS statistics. In this way, we need to solve the issue of statistical standard consistency of different data sources.

The BIS publishes two sets of statistics on the activity of internationally active banks: Locational statistics: detail the currency and geographical composition of banks' balance sheets according to the location of banks' offices (LBS). Consolidated statistics: detail banks' country risk exposures according to the nationality of banking groups (CBS). The BIS also publishes three sets of statistics on issuance in money and bond markets: international debt securities (IDS), domestic debt securities (DDS) and total debt securities (TDS). These statistics are harmonised with the Handbook on Securities Statistics[7], an internationally agreed framework for classifying debt securities issues. That is, the data that we want to use are come from

---

[6] IMF, Balance of payments and international investment position compilation guide, 2017.

[7] IMF, BIS and ECB, 2015, Handbook on securities statistics.

different data sources and different publishing agencies. Therefore, it is necessary to coordinate international agencies to develop common benchmarks and statistical ranges to avoid double calculation and omission.

By the uniform international statistical benchmark, we can use BDT to measure GFF, namely use Internet technology, the Internet of Things technology and statistical techniques to collect data, compile GFF statistics and release relevant information. To achieve this goal, we need to improve the environment of data transmission and prepare for three aspects. The first is the creation of a new international agreement on data transmission. It should be in conjunction with the relevant countries and international organizations formulate relevant international agreements about data transmission. The second is to improve the data transmission based on the uniform statistical benchmark. According to the relevant international agreements and the uniform statistical benchmark, the participating countries timely report relevant data to the IMF and other international organizations. The third is to strengthen the IMF's coordination and leadership in data transmission management. The international organizations collect and collate data by the procedures, and publish all kinds of data that meet the statistical benchmark in the online by the time limit.

4.3 The Expected Effect by Applying the BDT for Measuring GFF

Compared with the traditional statistics, the innovation of using BDT is based on intelligent sensor, information acquisition technology such as software device, in accordance with the requirements for large systems interconnection, build a system of information standardization, which include data transmission, statistics processing, and an information official announcement such a statistical information standardization. This will have the following effect for establishing GFF statistics.

4.3.1 Will enhance Data quality and financial supervision

The rapid development of the Internet has not only made it easier for countries to report their data to international organizations such as IMF, but also greatly expanded the amount of data held by international organizations. In addition, makes the IMF and other international organizations can be collated information and timely feedback to the world, to meet the demand for statistical information at all levels. By using BDT the statistical error of data transmission and processing can be reduced and the data quality can be improved. The application of high-quality GFF statistics can increase the controllability of financial risks, and timely discover and solve possible financial risk points. It is more accurate to grasp the regularity of financial risk and improve the financial supervision level of policy authorities.

4.3.2 Will reduce the asymmetry of the financial transaction information

So far, in the international financial market, due to the time, place and the borders of physical and institutional constraints, the transmission of financial data were slow; the demand of financial information is far greater than the supply. However, in the era of network financial,

financial data transmission will be improved, and data processing will be more quickly, it will be able to meet the balance of the financial information needs and supply.

4.3.3   High efficiency for Measuring GFF

Using the BDT to compile financial data is efficient, many processes and actions have completed in the online, and some action is automatic. At the right time, the right place, provide the necessary financial information to the appropriate information users in the appropriate manner. At present, the lag period of some financial information disclosure is too long, such as the CDIS data released the lag period of about 1 years, the CPIS and FD data released lag period of about 6 months. If we use BDT into the compilation of financial statistics will undoubtedly improve the efficiency of data transmission and consolidation. At the same time, strong data analysis ability can do high efficiency analysis of financial transactions and the market.

5.   Concluding Remarks

This paper discussed how to establish the GFF statistical framework, data collection sources, compared and integrated different data sources, and analyzed the possibility of using BDT to compile GFF statistics. In particular, the paper also discussed how to use BDT in financial statistics including GFF statistics, and its effects.

The paper has explored the following issues which are statistical agencies such as IMF and BIS how to measure CDIS, CPIS, FD, CBS and Reserve Assets which in National Accounts, Balance of Payments statistics, International Investment Position and financial statistics. Put forward the idea of applying BDT to compile GFF statistics. There are also need to address the innovations in data collection, compilation or reporting, and how are Big Data techniques being used to build a new statistical benchmark to measure the global flow of funds in macroeconomic and financial statistics. The policy recommendations for this paper are as follows.

(1) With the development of Internet technology, international financial transactions will become more and more rapid and the volume of transactions will become more and larger. In order to prevent financial risks, it is necessary to establish a GFF statistical system.

(2) To this end, we need to establish data transmission standards for the use big data technologies between international organizations such as the IMF and BIS and the participating countries.

(3) Based on the common statistical benchmarks, establish a network data transmission agreement for measuring GFF between the Member States and international organizations such as the IMF, which including direct investment, portfolio investment, financial derivatives, other investment and foreign currency reserve assets, etc.. It also should be clarified the deadline of reporting national data and the timing of the release of the IMF data; in the form of W-to-W; implement the system of information sharing.

References

[1] Bank for International Settlements, http://www.bis.org/statistics/consstats.htm. Sep. 5, 2017.

[2] Established Principal Global Indicators (PGI) Website:
http://www.principalglobalindicators.org/default.aspx, Sep. 10, 2016.

[3] European Communities, International Monetary Fund, Organisation for Economic Co-operation and Development, United Nations and World Bank, *System of National Account 2008,* Sales No. E.08.XVII.29, United Nations, New York (2009).

[4] Financial Stability Board and International Monetary Fund "The Financial Crisis and Information Gaps", Report to the G-20 Finance Ministers and Central Bank Governors (2009).

[5] GLobal Pulse, Big Data for Development: Opportunities and Challenges (White p. by Letouzé, E.). New York: United Nations (2012). Retrieved from
http://www.unglobalpulse.org/projects/BigDataforDevelopment, July 4, 2017.

[6] Hilbert, M. Big Data for Development: A Review of Promises and Challenges. Development Policy Review, 34(1), pp. 135–174 (2016).
http://doi.org/10.1111/dpr.12142 June 20,2017.

[7] IMF, Balance of payments and international investment position manual, 6th Edition (BPM6) (2014).

[8] −, http://www.imf.org/external/data.htm

[9] −, http://data.imf.org/?sk=40313609-F037-48C1-84B1-E1F1CE54D6D5&ss=139355280 3658

[10] −, http://data.imf.org/?sk=B981B4E3-4E58-467E-9B90-9DE0C3367363

[11] −, Update of the Monetary and Financial Statistics Manual (MFSM) and the Monetary and Financial Statistics Compilation Guide (MFSCG) (2016).

[12] −, Balance of Payments and International Investment Position Compilation Guide (2017).

[13] IMF, BIS and ECB, Handbook on securities statistics (2015).
http://www.imf.org/external/np/sta/wgsd/pdf/hss.pdf. March 10, 2017

[14] Luca Errico, Richard Walton, Alicia Hierro, Hanan AbuShanab, Goran Amidzic, "Global Flow of Funds: Mapping Bilateral Geographic Flows," Proceedings 59th ISI World Statistics Congress, 2825-2830 (2013).

[15] Luca Errico, Artak Harutyunyan, Elena Loukoianova, Richard Walton, Yevgeniya Korniyenko, Goran Amidžić, Hanan AbuShanab, Hyun Song Shin, "Mapping the Shadow Banking System Through a Global Flow of Funds Analysis," IMF Working Paper, WP/14/10, (2014).

[16] Manik Shrestha, Reimund Mink, and Segismundo Fassler, "An Integrated Framework for Financial Positions and Flows on a From-Whom-to-Whom Basis: Concepts, Status, and Prospects," IMF Working Paper WP/12/57 (2012).

[17] Nan Zhang, "New Frameworks for Measuring Global-Flow-of-Funds: Financial Stability in China", in the 32nd General Conference of The International Association for Research in

Income and Wealth (IARIW) (2012).

[18] ―, Measuring Global Flow of Funds and Integrating Real and Financial Accounts, Working paper, 2015 IARIW-OECD Conference: W(h)ither the SNA? April 16-17, 2015. http://www.iariw.org/c2015oecd.php

[19] Robert Heath and Evrim Bese Goksu, Financial Stability Analysis: What are the Data Needs? IMF Working Paper, WP/17/153 (2017).

[20] Sadao Ishida, *Flow of Funds in Japanese Economy*, Toyo Keizai Shimpo-Sha, 170-205, 1993.

[21] Shrestha, Manik, Reimund Mink and Segismundo Fassler, "An Integrated Framework for Financial Positions and Flows on a From-Whom-to-Whom Basis: Concepts, Status, and Prospects," IMF Working Paper WP/12/57 (2012).

[22] WEF (World Economic Forum), & Vital Wave Consulting, Big Data, Big Impact: New Possibilities for International Development. World Economic Forum. Retrieved August 24, 2012.
http://www.weforum.org/reports/big-data-big-impact-new-possibilities-international-development

[23] Zhang, N., The Global Flow of Funds Analysis in Theory and Application, Minerva-Shobo, pp. 31-67 (2005).

[24] ―, "New Frameworks for Measuring Global-Flow-of-Funds: Financial Stability in China," the 32nd General Conference of The International Association for Research in Income and Wealth (IARIW), http://www.iariw.org/c2012.php, Aug. 20, 2012.

[25] ―, "Measuring Global Flow of Funds: Theoretical Framework, Data Sources and Approaches" Kyushu University Press, pp. 47-60 (2016).

Chapter 4

Some Conjectures Concerning Irreducible Components of Harmonic Polynomials in the Case of $\mathfrak{so}(d,2)$

Ryoko Wada and *Yoshio Agaoka*
*Faculty of Economic Sciences, Hiroshima Shudo University,
1-1 Ozuka-Higashi 1-chome, Asaminami-Ku, Hiroshima, Japan 731-3195,
**Department of Mathematics, Graduate School of Science, Hiroshima University,
7-1 Kagamiyama 1-chome, Higashi-Hiroshima, Japan 739-8521.

Abstract

In the paper of Kostant-Rallis, classical harmonic polynomials on $\mathbf{C}^d$ are generalized to several vector spaces from the Lie algebraic viewpoint. In their formulation, the classical case $\mathbf{C}^d$ corresponds to the real rank 1 Lie algebra $\mathfrak{so}(d,1)$. In the series of papers we further investigate harmonic polynomials corresponding to remaining real rank 1 Lie algebras: $\mathfrak{su}(p,1)$, $\mathfrak{sp}(p,1)$, $\mathfrak{f}_{4(-20)}$, etc. In this paper we treat the case of real rank 2 Lie algebra $\mathfrak{so}(d,2)$. We give some new conjectures concerning the generators of irreducible components of lower part harmonic polynomials for the case $\mathfrak{so}(d,2)$.

Key Words:
Harmonic polynomial, Spherical harmonics, Reproducing kernel, Special function

1. Introduction

This paper is a continuation of our previous studies [8], [9], [10], [11].

Let $\mathfrak{g}$ be a complex semisimple Lie algebra and let $\mathfrak{g}_{\mathbf{R}}$ be a noncompact real form of $\mathfrak{g}$. We fix a maximal compact subalgebra $\mathfrak{k}_{\mathbf{R}}$ of $\mathfrak{g}_{\mathbf{R}}$, and let $\mathfrak{g}_{\mathbf{R}} = \mathfrak{k}_{\mathbf{R}} + \mathfrak{p}_{\mathbf{R}}$ be a Cartan decomposition of $\mathfrak{g}_{\mathbf{R}}$. We denote by $\mathfrak{g} = \mathfrak{k} + \mathfrak{p}$ its complexification.

In [6], [7] we considered the reproducing formulas of the harmonic polynomials in the cases where $\mathfrak{g}_{\mathbf{R}}$'s are of real rank 1. In [8] we began to study the case of classical Lie algebra $\mathfrak{g}_{\mathbf{R}} = \mathfrak{so}(d,2)$, which is of real rank 2. In the series of papers [8], [9], [10], [11] we settled several problems such as:

- Prove the structure theorem of the $\mathfrak{k}_{\mathbf{R}}$-irreducible decomposition of the space of polynomials on $\mathfrak{p}$.

- Give the formal $\mathfrak{k}_{\mathbf{R}}$-irreducible decomposition of the space of harmonic polynomials of general degree. (Here, a formal decomposition means a character level decomposition.)

• Give the explicit form of the generators of "principal" irreducible components of the space of polynomials (which are automatically harmonic).

• Give an algorithm to obtain generators of irreducible lower part components of the space of harmonic polynomials.

• Give the explicit decomposition and generators of lower parts up to degree 5.

• Give partial conjectures concerning the explicit form of the generators of lower irreducible components of harmonic polynomials.

• Give some examples of reproducing formulas of harmonic polynomials of degree ≤ 4.

• Give the reproducing formulas of the principal part of the spaces of harmonic polynomials of degree ≤ 5.

In this paper we give new conjectures concerning the generator of the irreducible component of lower part harmonic polynomials (Conjecture 4.1). Further, in the last section, we give examples of reproducing kernels of principal part of harmonic polynomials of special type for general degree.

2. Preliminaries

In this section we fix several notations. For details, see our previous papers [8], [9], [10], [11].

Let $\mathfrak{g} = \mathfrak{so}(d + 2, \mathbf{C})$ with $d \geq 4$, and $\mathfrak{g}_{\mathbf{R}} = \mathfrak{so}(d, 2)$ its real form. We set

$$\mathfrak{k} = \left\{ \begin{pmatrix} A & 0 \\ 0 & B \end{pmatrix} \in M(d + 2, \mathbf{C}) \; ; \; A \in \mathfrak{so}(d, \mathbf{C}), \; B \in \mathfrak{so}(2, \mathbf{C}) \right\},$$

$$\mathfrak{p} = \left\{ \begin{pmatrix} 0 & X \\ {}^t X & 0 \end{pmatrix} \in M(d + 2, \mathbf{C}) \; ; \; X \text{ is a complex } d \times 2 \text{ matrix} \right\},$$

$$K_{\mathbf{R}} = \left\{ \mathrm{Ad} \begin{pmatrix} A & 0 \\ 0 & B \end{pmatrix} \; ; \; A \in SO(d), \; B \in SO(2) \right\}.$$

Then we have $\mathfrak{g} = \mathfrak{k} + \mathfrak{p}$, and the group $K_{\mathbf{R}}$ acts on $\mathfrak{p}$ in the following way: For $\widetilde{X} = \begin{pmatrix} 0 & X \\ {}^t X & 0 \end{pmatrix} \in \mathfrak{p}$, and $g = \mathrm{Ad} \begin{pmatrix} A & 0 \\ 0 & B \end{pmatrix} \in K_{\mathbf{R}}$ ($A \in SO(d)$, $B \in SO(2)$) we set $g\widetilde{X} = \begin{pmatrix} 0 & AX^t B \\ {}^t(AX^t B) & 0 \end{pmatrix}$.

We denote by S_n the space of homogeneous polynomials on $\mathfrak{p}$ of degree n, where n is a non-negative integer.

For $\widetilde{X} = \begin{pmatrix} 0 & X \\ {}^t X & 0 \end{pmatrix} \in \mathfrak{p}$ with $X = (x \; y)$ $(x, y \in \mathbf{C}^d)$, we put $\begin{pmatrix} z \\ w \end{pmatrix} = \begin{pmatrix} x + iy \\ x - iy \end{pmatrix} \in$

$\mathbf{C}^{2d}$ and we define the linear bijective mapping $\Psi : \mathfrak{p} \longrightarrow \mathbf{C}^{2d}$ by $\Psi(\widetilde{X}) = \begin{pmatrix} z \\ w \end{pmatrix}$. We denote by $S_n(\mathbf{C}^{2d})$ the space of homogeneous polynomials on $\mathbf{C}^{2d}$ with degree n. We identify two spaces S_n and $S_n(\mathbf{C}^{2d})$ through the isomorphism Ψ.

The definition of harmonic polynomial on $\mathfrak{p}$ is given in [3], and through the above isomorphism Ψ, a polynomial $f(z_1, \cdots, z_d, w_1, \cdots, w_d) \in S_n(\mathbf{C}^{2d})$ is harmonic if and only if

$$\sum_i \frac{\partial^2 f}{\partial z_i \partial w_i} = 0, \qquad \sum_{i,j} \frac{\partial^2}{\partial z_i^2} \left(\frac{\partial^2 f}{\partial w_j^2} \right) = 0.$$

We denote by $\mathcal{H}_n$ the space of homogeneous harmonic polynomials of degree n on $\mathfrak{p}$, which is naturally identified with the space of homogeneous harmonic polynomials of degree n on $\mathbf{C}^{2d}$. For more details on harmonic polynomials of $\mathfrak{p}$, see [1], [3].

3. Irreducible Decomposition of S_n

In this section, we review the $K_{\mathbf{R}}$-irreducible decomposition of the space $\mathcal{H}_n$ and its generator. We use the same notations in [8], [9], [10], [11].

We first remark that $K_{\mathbf{R}}$ is naturally isomorphic to the product group $SO(d) \times SO(2)$, and acts on S_n and $\mathcal{H}_n$. For z, $w \in \mathbf{C}^d$ we put $z \cdot w = {}^t zw$, $z^2 = z \cdot z$, $w^2 = w \cdot w$. Then the natural action of the special orthogonal group $SO(d)$ on $\mathbf{C}^d$ preserves this product.

The $K_{\mathbf{R}}$-irreducible representation space is symbolically expressed as $(p\Lambda_1 + q\Lambda_2) \otimes V_k$, where p, q are non-negative integers and $k \in \mathbf{Z}$. We say that the irreducible component $(p\Lambda_1 + q\Lambda_2) \otimes V_k$ in S_n is *principal* if $p + 2q = n$, and is called a *lower* component if $p + 2q < n$.

We denote by P_n the direct sum of principal irreducible components of S_n, and by L_n the direct sum of subspaces of S_n consisting of lower components of S_n.

Lower components of S_n are obtained by a product of principal components and the following three polynomials

$$z^2, \quad z \cdot w, \quad w^2.$$

These are 1-dimensional irreducible subspaces of quadratic polynomials S_2, whose characters are respectively given by

$$(0) \otimes V_2, \quad (0) \otimes V_0, \quad (0) \otimes V_{-2}.$$

Then by making a tensor product of a principal component $(p\Lambda_1 + q\Lambda_2) \otimes V_k$ $(p + 2q = n - 2l)$ of S_{n-2l} $(0 < l \leq n/2)$ and an l-th product of the above three quadratic polynomials $(z^2)^s (z \cdot w)^t (w^2)^u$ $(s + t + u = l)$, we obtain a lower irreducible component $(p\Lambda_1 + q\Lambda_2) \otimes V_{k+2s-2u}$ in S_n. Any irreducible component of L_n can be obtained in this way.

The $K_{\mathbf{R}}$-irreducible decompositions of the principal part P_n is given by

$$P_n = \sum_{\substack{p+2q=n, \\ p \geq 0, q \geq 0}} (p\Lambda_1 + q\Lambda_2) \otimes (V_p + V_{p-2} + \cdots + V_{-(p-2)} + V_{-p}).$$

Remind that any polynomial in the principal component P_n is harmonic, and the multiplicity of any irreducible principal component is always 1 ([p.88; 10]). The generator of the principal irreducible component

$$(p\Lambda_1 + q\Lambda_2) \otimes V_k \subset P_n$$

with $p + 2q = n$ $(p \geq 0, q \geq 0)$, $|k| \leq p$ and $k \equiv p \pmod 2$ is given by

$$(z \cdot \alpha)^{(p+k)/2} (w \cdot \alpha)^{(p-k)/2} \{(z \cdot \alpha)(w \cdot \beta) - (z \cdot \beta)(w \cdot \alpha)\}^q$$

with $\alpha^2 = \alpha \cdot \beta = \beta^2 = 0$ (Theorem 4.1 of [11]). In other words, a polynomial

$$(z \cdot \alpha)^\lambda (w \cdot \alpha)^\nu \{(z \cdot \alpha)(w \cdot \beta) - (z \cdot \beta)(w \cdot \alpha)\}^\xi$$

with $\alpha^2 = \alpha \cdot \beta = \beta^2 = 0$ gives a generator of the principal irreducible component

$$((\lambda + \nu)\Lambda_1 + \xi\Lambda_2) \otimes V_{\lambda - \nu}$$

with degree $n = \lambda + \nu + 2\xi$.

Next, we consider the lower components. We express the lower harmonic components in $\mathcal{H}_n$ as $\mathcal{LH}_n$. Then we have the following $K_\mathbf{R}$-irreducible decomposition (cf. [p.97; 11]):

$$\mathcal{LH}_n = \sum_{\substack{p + 2q \leq n - 2, \\ p \geq 0, \, q \geq 0, \\ p \equiv n \,(\mathrm{mod}\, 2)}} (p\Lambda_1 + q\Lambda_2) \otimes (V_{n-2q} + V_{n-2q-2} + \cdots + V_{n-2p-2q} \\ + V_{-(n-2p-2q)} + \cdots + V_{-(n-2q-2)} + V_{-(n-2q)}).$$

The multiplicity of each irreducible component is at most 2, and the multiplicity 2 case occurs if and only if $p + 2q \leq n - 2$ and $p + q \geq n/2$ for the space V_k with $|k| \leq 2p + 2q - n$.

In the following arguments we decompose $\mathcal{LH}_n$ into two subspaces. We put

$$\mathcal{LH}_n^+ = \sum_{\substack{p + 2q \leq n - 2, \\ p \geq 0, \, q \geq 0, \\ p \equiv n \,(\mathrm{mod}\, 2)}} (p\Lambda_1 + q\Lambda_2) \otimes (V_{n-2q} + V_{n-2q-2} + \cdots + V_{n-2p-2q})$$

and

$$\mathcal{LH}_n^- = \sum_{\substack{p + 2q \leq n - 2, \\ p \geq 0, \, q \geq 0, \\ p \equiv n \,(\mathrm{mod}\, 2)}} (p\Lambda_1 + q\Lambda_2) \otimes (V_{-(n-2p-2q)} + \cdots + V_{-(n-2q-2)} + V_{-(n-2q)}).$$

Then, we formally obtain a direct sum decomposition $\mathcal{LH}_n = \mathcal{LH}_n^+ \oplus \mathcal{LH}_n^-$, whose two components are both multiplicity free. In the following we consider the problem to find a generator of each irreducible component of $\mathcal{LH}_n^+$. Generators of the remaining part $\mathcal{LH}_n^-$ can be obtained by changing the letters z and w in generators of $\mathcal{LH}_n^+$.

To find a generator, for later use, we review formulas to calculate two derivatives

$$\sum_i \frac{\partial^2 f}{\partial z_i \partial w_i}, \qquad \sum_{i,j} \frac{\partial^2}{\partial z_i^2}\left(\frac{\partial^2 f}{\partial w_j^2}\right)$$

for the polynomial of the form

$$f = F[s, t, u, \lambda, \nu, \xi] \\ = (z^2)^s (z \cdot w)^t (w^2)^u (z \cdot \alpha)^\lambda (w \cdot \alpha)^\nu \{(z \cdot \alpha)(w \cdot \beta) - (z \cdot \beta)(w \cdot \alpha)\}^\xi$$

with degree $n = 2s+2t+2u+\lambda+\nu+2\xi$. Remind that the polynomial $F[s,t,u,\lambda,\nu,\xi]$ gives a generator of the $SO(d) \times SO(2)$-irreducible component

$$((\lambda + \nu)\Lambda_1 + \xi\Lambda_2) \otimes V_{2s-2u+\lambda-\nu}$$

of S_n in case $\alpha^2 = \alpha \cdot \beta = \beta^2 = 0$. (It gives a generator of a principal part if and only if $s = t = u = 0$, as stated before.)

The above two derivatives of $f = F[s,t,u,\lambda,\nu,\xi]$ can be again expressed as a linear combination of $F[\bar{s}, \bar{t}, \bar{u}, \bar{\lambda}, \bar{\nu}, \bar{\xi}]$ for some $\bar{s}, \bar{t}, \bar{u}, \bar{\lambda}, \bar{\nu}, \bar{\xi}$ in the following way:

Proposition 3.1 ([p.103; 11]). *Assume $\alpha^2 = \alpha \cdot \beta = \beta^2 = 0$. Then we have the following formulas for $f = F[s,t,u,\lambda,\nu,\xi]$:*

$$\sum_i \frac{\partial^2 f}{\partial z_i \partial w_i} = 4su\, F[s-1,t+1,u-1,\lambda,\nu,\xi]$$
$$+ 2s\nu\, F[s-1,t,u,\lambda+1,\nu-1,\xi] + 2u\lambda\, F[s,t,u-1,\lambda-1,\nu+1,\xi]$$
$$+ t(d+2s+t+2u+\lambda+\nu+2\xi-1)\, F[s,t-1,u,\lambda,\nu,\xi],$$

$$\sum_{i,j} \frac{\partial^2}{\partial z_i^2}\left(\frac{\partial^2 f}{\partial w_j^2}\right)$$
$$= 4su(d+2s+2t+2\lambda+2\xi-2)(d+2t+2u+2\nu+2\xi-2)\, F[s-1,t,u-1,\lambda,\nu,\xi]$$
$$+ 4st\nu(d+2s+2t+2\lambda+2\xi-2)\, F[s-1,t-1,u,\lambda+1,\nu-1,\xi]$$
$$+ 4tu\lambda(d+2t+2u+2\nu+2\xi-2)\, F[s,t-1,u-1,\lambda-1,\nu+1,\xi]$$
$$+ 2t(t-1)[d(s+u+1)+2\{s(s+t+\lambda+\xi-1)+u(t+u+\nu+\xi-1)$$
$$+ (\lambda+1)(\nu+1)+t+\xi-3\}]\, F[s,t-2,u,\lambda,\nu,\xi]$$
$$+ 2t(t-1)(t-2)\lambda\, F[s+1,t-3,u,\lambda-1,\nu+1,\xi]$$
$$+ 2t(t-1)(t-2)\nu\, F[s,t-3,u+1,\lambda+1,\nu-1,\xi]$$
$$+ t(t-1)(t-2)(t-3)\, F[s+1,t-4,u+1,\lambda,\nu,\xi].$$

Now we express a generator of the m-th irreducible component of $\mathcal{LH}_n^+$ as a linear combination of $F[s,t,u,\lambda,\nu,\xi]$ as follows (cf. [p.108; 11]):

$$\sum_{i+2j \leq m-1} a_{ij}^m\, F[s_0-i-j+1,i,j,p-M_{ij},M_{ij},q] \in (p\Lambda_1 + q\Lambda_2) \otimes V_{n-2q-2(m-1)},$$

where $M_{ij} = m-i-2j-1$ ($i \geq 0$, $j \geq 0$, $i+2j \leq m-1$). Here a_{ij}^m's are coefficients, and s_0 is a non-negative integer defined by the equality $n = 2s_0+p+2q+2$. Remind that the integer m moves in the range $1 \leq m \leq p+1$. Since $p+2q \leq n-2$, we have the inequality $m+1 \leq p+2 \leq n$. In particular, we have $p-M_{ij} \geq p-(m-1) \geq 0$, and the m-th component appears only in the case $n \geq m+1$ with $p \geq m-1$. (In this paper, compared with the expression in [11], we change the letter s to s_0 to avoid confusion. The integer s_0 is a fixed constant defined by n, p and q, while the integer s moves freely in the range $s \geq 0$.)

Then, applying Proposition 3.1, we can express a condition of the harmonicity of the above polynomial as a system of linear equations on coefficients a_{ij}^m as follows:

Proposition 3.2. *We put*

$$f = \sum_{i+2j \leq m-1} a_{ij}^m \, F[s_0 - i - j + 1, i, j, p - M_{ij}, M_{ij}, q] \in (p\Lambda_1 + q\Lambda_2) \otimes V_{n-2q-2(m-1)}.$$

Then,

(1) *f satisfies*

$$\sum_i \frac{\partial^2 f}{\partial z_i \partial w_i} = 0$$

if and only if

$$4(s_0 - i - j + 1)(j+1)\, a_{i-1,j+1}^m + 2(s_0 - i - j + 1)M_{ij}\, a_{ij}^m$$
$$+ 2(j+1)(p - M_{ij} + 2)\, a_{i,j+1}^m + (i+1)(2s_0 + p + 2q + d - i)\, a_{i+1,j}^m = 0.$$

Here, (i,j) is a pair of non-negative integers satisfying $i+2j \leq m-2$. Exceptionally, in case $i + 2j = m - 2$, we must exclude the third term in the above sum. Also we assume $a_{-1,j+1}^m = 0$ in the first term in case $i = 0$.

(2) *f satisfies*

$$\sum_{i,j} \frac{\partial^2}{\partial z_i^2} \left(\frac{\partial^2 f}{\partial w_j^2} \right) = 0$$

if and onlt if

$$4(s_0 - i - j)(j+1)(d + 2s_0 + 2p + 2q - 2m + 2i + 2j + 4)(d + 2q + 2m - 2j - 6)\, a_{i,j+1}^m$$
$$+ 4(s_0 - i - j)(i+1)(M_{ij} - 1)(d + 2s_0 + 2p + 2q - 2m + 2i + 2j + 4)\, a_{i+1,j}^m$$
$$+ 4(i+1)(j+1)(p - M_{ij} + 3)(d + 2q + 2m - 2j - 6)\, a_{i+1,j+1}^m$$
$$+ 2(i+2)(i+1)[d(s_0 - i) + 2\{(s_0 - i - j - 1)(s_0 + p + q + i + j - m + 3)$$
$$+ j(q + m - j - 2) + (p - M_{ij} + 3)(M_{ij} - 1) + i + q - 1\}]\, a_{i+2,j}^m$$
$$+ 2(i+3)(i+2)(i+1)(p - M_{ij} + 3)\, a_{i+3,j}^m$$
$$+ 2(i+3)(i+2)(i+1)(M_{ij} - 1)\, a_{i+3,j-1}^m$$
$$+ (i+4)(i+3)(i+2)(i+1)\, a_{i+4,j-1}^m = 0.$$

In this case, (i,j) is a pair of non-negative integers satisfying $i + 2j \leq m - 3$, and exceptionally, in case $i + 2j = m - 3$, we must exclude the third and the fifth terms in the above sum. In addition we assume $a_{i+3,-1}^m = a_{i+4,-1}^m = 0$ in the sixth and the seventh (=the last) terms in case $j = 0$.

The number of coefficients a_{ij}^m $(i + 2j \leq m - 1)$ is equal to

$$\begin{cases} (l+1)^2 & (m = 2l+1), \\ l(l+1) & (m = 2l). \end{cases}$$

On the other hand, the number of the equations in (1) is equal to

$$\begin{cases} l(l+1) & (m = 2l+1), \\ l^2 & (m = 2l), \end{cases}$$

and the number of the equations in (2) is equal to

$$\begin{cases} l^2 & (m = 2l+1), \\ l(l-1) & (m = 2l). \end{cases}$$

Hence, the above system of linear equations on a_{ij}^m is overdetermined in case $m \geq 5$.

Proof. We here give an outline of the proof of (1). The result (2) can be verified in the same way by some calculations.

First, by applying Proposition 3.1, we calculate

$$\sum_i \frac{\partial^2 f}{\partial z_i \partial w_i}$$

for

$$f = \sum_{i+2j \leq m-1} a_{ij}^m F[s_0 - i - j + 1, i, j, p - M_{ij}, M_{ij}, q].$$

Then, it is equal to

$$\sum_{i+2j \leq m-1} a_{ij}^m \{ 4(s_0 - i - j + 1)j\, F[s_0 - i - j, i+1, j-1, p - M_{ij}, M_{ij}, q]$$
$$+ 2(s_0 - i - j + 1)M_{ij}\, F[s_0 - i - j, i, j, p - M_{ij} + 1, M_{ij} - 1, q]$$
$$+ 2j(p - M_{ij})\, F[s_0 - i - j + 1, i, j - 1, p - M_{ij} - 1, M_{ij} + 1, q]$$
$$+ i(2s_0 + p + 2q + d - i + 1)\, F[s_0 - i - j + 1, i - 1, j, p - M_{ij}, M_{ij}, q] \}.$$

We re-express this sum as a linear combination of the polynomial of the form

$$F[s_0 - i - j, i, j, p - M_{ij} + 1, M_{ij} - 1, q].$$

For example, for the first term in the sum, we replace i and j by $i - 1$ and $j + 1$, respectively. Then, it becomes

$$a_{i-1,j+1}^m \times 4(s_0 - i - j + 1)(j + 1)\, F[s_0 - i - j, i, j, p - M_{ij} + 1, M_{ij} - 1, q].$$

In this expression, (i, j) must satisfy $i + 2j \leq m - 2$ and $i \geq 1$. Similarly, for the third and the fourth term in the sum, we replace i and j suitably. Then finally, the coefficient of $F[s_0 - i - j, i, j, p - M_{ij} + 1, M_{ij} - 1, q]$ in the sum becomes

$$4(s_0 - i - j + 1)(j + 1)\, a_{i-1,j+1}^m + 2(s_0 - i - j + 1)M_{ij}\, a_{ij}^m$$
$$+ 2(j + 1)(p - M_{ij} + 2)\, a_{i,j+1}^m + (i + 1)(2s_0 + p + 2q + d - i)\, a_{i+1,j}^m,$$

under the restrictions on (i, j) stated in the proposition.   q.e.d.

4. New Conjectures on Lower Harmonic Polynomials

We use the same notations as before. The generator of the m-th irreducible component of $\mathcal{LH}_n^+$ can be expressed in the form

$$\sum_{i+2j \leq m-1} a_{ij}^m F[s_0 - i - j + 1, i, j, p - M_{ij}, M_{ij}, q] \in (p\Lambda_1 + q\Lambda_2) \otimes V_{n-2q-2(m-1)}.$$

We conjecture that the ratio of the coefficients a_{ij}^m is uniquely determined by the equations in Proposition 3.2, and by examining a vast amount of explicit examples, we finally arrive at the following main Conjecture of the paper.

Conjecture 4.1. *Up to a non-zero common constant, the coefficient a_{ij}^m is given by*

$$a_{ij}^m = (-1)^i \sum_{\left\{ \begin{array}{c} \sigma + 2\tau \leq M_{ij} \\ i \geq \sigma \geq 0 \\ \tau \geq 0 \end{array} \right.} \frac{2^{i+j+\sigma}}{(i-\sigma)!\,j!\,\sigma!\,\tau!\,(M_{ij}-\sigma-2\tau)!} \prod_{v=1}^{i+j} (s_0 - v + 2)$$

$$\times \prod_{v=1}^{\tau} (s_0 - j - \sigma - \tau + v + 1) \prod_{v=1}^{\sigma} (s_0 + p - m + i + j - v + 4)$$

$$\times \prod_{v=\sigma+\tau+1}^{[\frac{m-2j-1}{2}]} (d + 2q + 2j + 2v - 4) \prod_{v=1}^{j} (d + s_0 + p + 2q + v - 2)$$

$$\times \prod_{v=1}^{M_{ij}-\sigma-2\tau} (d + 2s_0 + p + 2q + i - \sigma + v - 1)$$

$$\times \prod_{v=1}^{\tau} (d + 2s_0 + 2p + 2q + 2i - 2\sigma - 2\tau + 2v).$$

This is a polynomial of d with degree

$$M_{ij} + \left[\frac{m-1}{2}\right] = \begin{cases} 3l - i - 2j & (m = 2l+1), \\ 3l - i - 2j - 2 & (m = 2l). \end{cases}$$

In the previous paper [p.108; 11] we state a conjecture on a_{ij}^m in the case $m = 2l+1$. The coefficient a_{ij}^m in Conjecture 4.1 coincides with a_{ij}^m given in [p.108; 11] multiplied by the constant $2^{m-1}/(m-1)!$.

On account of the first component $s_0 - i - j + 1$ in $F[s_0 - i - j + 1, i, j, p - M_{ij}, M_{ij}, q]$, two integers i and j must satisfy the inequality $i + j \leq s_0 + 1$. But we may drop this condition because the coefficient a_{ij}^m in Conjecture 4.1 contains the product term $\prod_{v=1}^{i+j}(s_0 - v + 2)$. This term becomes 0 in case $i + j \geq s_0 + 2$. Thus we may consider $a_{ij}^m = 0$ in this case, and the term $a_{ij}^m F[s_0 - i - j + 1, i, j, p - M_{ij}, M_{ij}, q]$ does not appear in case $i + j \geq s_0 + 2$.

By using computers, we verified Conjecture 4.1 for the cases $1 \leq m \leq 9$. The expression of a_{ij}^m in this conjecture is quite complicated. But in the special case $M_{ij} = 0$, i.e., the case $i + 2j = m - 1$, the above sum is taken only for the case $\sigma = \tau = 0$, and as a result, a_{ij}^m can be expressed as a product of linear forms:

$$a_{ij}^m = (-1)^i \frac{2^{i+j}}{i!\,j!} \prod_{v=1}^{i+j} (s_0 - v + 2) \prod_{v=1}^{[\frac{i}{2}]} (d + 2q + 2j + 2v - 4)$$

$$\times \prod_{v=1}^{j} (d + s_0 + p + 2q + v - 2).$$

The same phenomenon occurs in the case $M_{ij} = 1$ and $i = 0$. In this case we have $m = 2j + 2$, and

$$a_{0j}^m = \frac{2^j}{j!} \prod_{v=1}^{j} (s_0 - v + 2) \prod_{v=1}^{j} (d + s_0 + p + 2q + v - 2)(d + 2s_0 + p + 2q).$$

But in general, a_{ij}^m becomes a quite lengthy polynomial of d, s_0, p, q, if we actually expand the product in Conjecture 4.1. We now consider that the expression of a_{ij}^m in Conjecture 4.1 is the most natural expression representing a_{ij}^m.

We here give some examples for small m that are already verified by using computers:

$m = 1$

$$a_{00}^1 = 1.$$

$m = 2$

$$a_{00}^2 = d + 2s_0 + p + 2q,$$
$$a_{10}^2 = -2(s_0 + 1).$$

$m = 3$

$$a_{00}^3 = \frac{1}{2}(d + 2q - 2)(d + 2s_0 + p + 2q)(d + 2s_0 + p + 2q + 1)$$
$$+ (s_0 + 1)(d + 2s_0 + 2p + 2q),$$
$$a_{10}^3 = -2(s_0 + 1)(d + 2q - 2)(d + 2s_0 + p + 2q + 1)$$
$$- 4(s_0 + 1)(s_0 + p + 1),$$
$$a_{20}^3 = 2(s_0 + 1)s_0(d + 2q - 2),$$
$$a_{01}^3 = 2(s_0 + 1)(d + s_0 + p + 2q - 1).$$

$m = 4$

$$a_{00}^4 = \frac{1}{6}(d + 2q - 2)(d + 2s_0 + p + 2q)(d + 2s_0 + p + 2q + 1)(d + 2s_0 + p + 2q + 2)$$
$$+ (s_0 + 1)(d + 2s_0 + p + 2q)(d + 2s_0 + 2p + 2q),$$
$$a_{10}^4 = -(s_0 + 1)(d + 2q - 2)(d + 2s_0 + p + 2q + 1)(d + 2s_0 + p + 2q + 2)$$
$$- 4(s_0 + 1)(s_0 + p)(d + 2s_0 + p + 2q)$$
$$- 2(s_0 + 1)^2(d + 2s_0 + 2p + 2q + 2),$$
$$a_{20}^4 = 2(s_0 + 1)s_0(d + 2q - 2)(d + 2s_0 + p + 2q + 2)$$
$$+ 8(s_0 + 1)s_0(s_0 + p + 1),$$
$$a_{30}^4 = -\frac{4}{3}(s_0 + 1)s_0(s_0 - 1)(d + 2q - 2),$$
$$a_{01}^4 = 2(s_0 + 1)(d + s_0 + p + 2q - 1)(d + 2s_0 + p + 2q),$$
$$a_{11}^4 = -4(s_0 + 1)s_0(d + s_0 + p + 2q - 1).$$

The result $a_{00}^1 = 1$ in the case $m = 1$ implies that $F[s_0 + 1, 0, 0, p, 0, q] \in (p\Lambda_1 + q\Lambda_2) \otimes V_{n-2q}$ gives a generator of the first term of $\mathcal{LH}_n^+$, where $n = 2s_0 + p + 2q + 2$.

In case $n \geq 3$ the second term actually appears and the above result for the case $m = 2$ implies that it is generated by

$$(d + 2s_0 + p + 2q)F[s_0 + 1, 0, 0, p - 1, 1, q] - 2(s_0 + 1)F[s_0, 1, 0, p, 0, q]$$
$$\in (p\Lambda_1 + q\Lambda_2) \otimes V_{n-2q-2}.$$

For the third term $(m = 3)$ the polynomial

$$f = a_{00}^3 F[s_0 + 1, 0, 0, p - 2, 2, q] + a_{10}^3 F[s_0, 1, 0, p - 1, 1, q] + a_{20}^3 F[s_0 - 1, 2, 0, p, 0, q]$$
$$+ a_{01}^3 F[s_0, 0, 1, p, 0, q] \in (p\Lambda_1 + q\Lambda_2) \otimes V_{n-2q-4}$$

with $n \geq 4$ and $p \geq 2$ is harmonic if and only if

$$\begin{cases} 4(s_0 + 1)\, a_{00}^3 + (d + 2s_0 + p + 2q)\, a_{10}^3 + 2p\, a_{01}^3 = 0, \\ s_0\, a_{10}^3 + (d + 2s_0 + p + 2q - 1)\, a_{20}^3 + 2s_0\, a_{01}^3 = 0, \\ s_0(d + 2s_0 + 2p + 2q - 2)\{a_{10}^3 + a_{20}^3 + (d + 2q)\, a_{01}^3\} = 0 \end{cases} \tag{4.1}$$

in case $s_0 \geq 1$. The first two conditions follow from the second derivative of f, and the third one follows from the fourth derivative of f. From these three equations we can uniquely determine the ratio $a_{00}^3 : a_{10}^3 : a_{20}^3 : a_{01}^3$, which is given in the above list. (In actual calculations we used computers. See also [p.105; 11].) The multiplicity of $(p\Lambda_1 + q\Lambda_2) \otimes V_{n-2q-4}$ in $\mathcal{LH}_n$ is 1 in case $s_0 \geq 1$. Hence we may say that the above f gives a generator of $(p\Lambda_1 + q\Lambda_2) \otimes V_{n-2q-4}$ in $\mathcal{LH}_n^+$.

But the situation completely differs in case $s_0 = 0$. In this case among three equations in (4.1), the second and the third equations reduce to trivial equations, and the ratio $a_{00}^3 : a_{10}^3 : a_{01}^3$ is not uniquely determined. (Note that in this case the coefficient a_{20}^3 does not appear since $i + j \geq s_0 + 2$, or we may set $a_{20}^3 = 0$ as stated before.)

In the case $s_0 = 0$ the multiplicity of $(p\Lambda_1 + q\Lambda_2) \otimes V_{n-2q-4}$ in $\mathcal{LH}_n$ is 2, and we have actually obtain two generators of this space from the first equation in (4.1). To obtain a canonical generator of $(p\Lambda_1 + q\Lambda_2) \otimes V_{n-2q-4}$ in $\mathcal{LH}_n^+$, we adopt the solution a_{ij}^m which we obtained in the case $s_0 \geq 1$, and substitute $s_0 = 0$ into all a_{ij}^m's. (See the explanation stated in [p.105~; 11].) Note that the solution a_{ij}^m of (4.1) in case $s_0 \geq 1$ clearly satisfies the first equation of (4.1) after substituting $s_0 = 0$, and so we may adopt it as a generator of $(p\Lambda_1 + q\Lambda_2) \otimes V_{n-2q-4}$ in $\mathcal{LH}_n^+$ common to all $s_0 \geq 0$. In case $s_0 = 0$ it is explicitly given by

$$f = a_{00}^3 F[1, 0, 0, p - 2, 2, q] + a_{10}^3 F[0, 1, 0, p - 1, 1, q] + a_{01}^3 F[0, 0, 1, p, 0, q]$$
$$\in (p\Lambda_1 + q\Lambda_2) \otimes V_{n-2q-4}$$

with

$$\begin{cases} a_{00}^3 = \frac{1}{2}(d + 2q - 2)(d + p + 2q)(d + p + 2q + 1) + (d + 2p + 2q), \\ a_{10}^3 = -2(d + 2q - 2)(d + p + 2q + 1) - 4(p + 1), \\ a_{01}^3 = 2(d + p + 2q - 1). \end{cases}$$

Note that since $s_0 = 0$, we have $n = p + 2q + 2$. In particular we have $n - 2q - 4 = p - 2$.

On the other hand, a canonical generator of $(p\Lambda_1 + q\Lambda_2) \otimes V_{n-2q-4}$ in $\mathcal{LH}_n^-$ can be obtained in the following way: In general, by changing the letters z and w in the generator of the space $(p\Lambda_1 + q\Lambda_2) \otimes V_k$ in $\mathcal{LH}_n$, we have a generator of the space $(p\Lambda_1 + q\Lambda_2) \otimes V_{-k}$ in $\mathcal{LH}_n$. Now, we can obtain a generator of the $(p+1)$-th $(=$ the last) component $(p\Lambda_1 + q\Lambda_2) \otimes V_{-p+2}$ in $\mathcal{LH}_n^+$ by applying Conjecture 4.1. (Note that $n - 2q - 2\{(p+1) - 1\} = -p + 2$.) Then, by changing the letters z and w, we obtain another generator of the space $(p\Lambda_1 + q\Lambda_2) \otimes V_{p-2}$ in $\mathcal{LH}_n$. We consider it as a generator of the space $(p\Lambda_1 + q\Lambda_2) \otimes V_{p-2}$ in $\mathcal{LH}_n^-$.

As one example, we consider the case $n = 5$, $p = 3$ and $q = 0$ (see [p.105$\sim$; 11].) In this case the generator of the space $(3\Lambda_1) \otimes V_1$ in $\mathcal{LH}_5^+$ is given by

$$f = a_{00}^3 \, F[1,0,0,1,2,0] + a_{10}^3 \, F[0,1,0,2,1,0] + a_{01}^3 \, F[0,0,1,3,0,0]$$

with

$$\begin{cases} a_{00}^3 = \frac{1}{2}(d-2)(d+3)(d+4) + (d+6) = \frac{1}{2}(d+2)(d^2+3d-6), \\ a_{10}^3 = -2(d-2)(d+4) - 16 = -2d(d+2), \\ a_{01}^3 = 2(d+2). \end{cases}$$

Hence this space is generated by

$$f = (d^2+3d-6) \, F[1,0,0,1,2,0] - 4d \, F[0,1,0,2,1,0] + 4 \, F[0,0,1,3,0,0].$$

Next we consider the 4-th component $(3\Lambda_1) \otimes V_{-1}$ in $\mathcal{LH}_5^+$. We substitute $p = 3$, $q = 0$ and $s_0 = 0$ to the list for the case $m = 4$. Then we have

$$\begin{cases} a_{00}^4 = \frac{1}{6}(d-2)(d+3)(d+4)(d+5) + (d+3)(d+6) \\ \quad = \frac{1}{6}(d+2)(d+3)(d^2+5d-2), \\ a_{10}^4 = -(d-2)(d+4)(d+5) - 12(d+3) - 2(d+8) = -(d+2)^2(d+3), \\ a_{01}^4 = 2(d+2)(d+3), \end{cases}$$

and remaining a_{ij}^4's are 0. Thus, it is generated by

$$(d^2+5d-2) \, F[1,0,0,0,3,0] - 6(d+2) \, F[0,1,0,1,2,0] + 12 \, F[0,0,1,2,1,0].$$

Therefore, by changing the letters z and w, it follows that the generator of $(3\Lambda_1) \otimes V_1$ in $\mathcal{LH}_5^-$ is given by

$$12 \, F[1,0,0,1,2,0] - 6(d+2) \, F[0,1,0,2,1,0] + (d^2+5d-2) \, F[0,0,1,3,0,0].$$

It is easy to see that these two generators of $(3\Lambda_1) \otimes V_1$ in $\mathcal{LH}_5^\pm$ are linearly independent since $d \geq 4$.

Next, we consider the fourth term $(m = 4)$. The polynomial

$$f = a_{00}^4 \, F[s_0+1,0,0,p-3,3,q] + a_{10}^4 \, F[s_0,1,0,p-2,2,q] + a_{20}^4 \, F[s_0-1,2,0,p-1,1,q]$$
$$+ a_{30}^4 \, F[s_0-2,3,0,p,0,q] + a_{01}^4 \, F[s_0,0,1,p-1,1,q] + a_{11}^4 \, F[s_0-1,1,1,p,0,q]$$
$$\in (p\Lambda_1 + q\Lambda_2) \otimes V_{n-2q-6}$$

with $n \geq 5$ and $p \geq 3$ is harmonic if and only if

$$
\left\{
\begin{array}{l}
6(s_0 + 1)a_{00}^4 + (d + 2s_0 + p + 2q)a_{10}^4 + 2(p - 1)a_{01}^4 = 0, \\
2s_0 a_{01}^4 + (d + 2s_0 + p + 2q)a_{11}^4 = 0, \\
2s_0 a_{10}^4 + (d + 2s_0 + p + 2q - 1)a_{20}^4 + 2s_0 a_{01}^4 + pa_{11}^4 = 0, \\
2(s_0 - 1)a_{20}^4 + 3(d + 2s_0 + p + 2q - 2)a_{30}^4 + 4(s_0 - 1)a_{11}^4 = 0, \\
2s_0(d + 2s_0 + 2p + 2q - 4)a_{10}^4 + \{s_0(d + 2q - 6) + 2(s_0 + 1)(s_0 + p)\}a_{20}^4 + 3pa_{30}^4 \\
\qquad + s_0(d + 2q + 2)(d + 2s_0 + 2p + 2q - 4)a_{01}^4 + p(d + 2q + 2)a_{11}^4 = 0, \\
(s_0 - 1)(d + 2s_0 + 2p + 2q - 2)\{2a_{20}^4 + 3a_{30}^4 + (d + 2q + 2)a_{11}^4\} = 0
\end{array}
\right.
$$

in case $s_0 \geq 2$. The first four conditions follow from the second derivative of f, and the last two conditions follow from the fourth derivative of f. In contrast to the cases $m \leq 3$, the above system looks like a determined system consisting of six indeterminants and six equations. But actually they contain only five independent equations, and the ratio $a_{00}^4 : a_{10}^4 : a_{20}^4 : a_{30}^4 : a_{01}^4 : a_{11}^4$ is uniquely determined, as listed before. This gives a generator of $(p\Lambda_1 + q\Lambda_2) \otimes V_{n-2q-6}$ in $\mathcal{LH}_n^+$.

In case $s_0 = 1$ we have $a_{ij}^4 = 0$ for $i + j \geq 3$. Hence the fourth and the last equations reduce to trivial conditions. By direct calculations we know that the remaining four equations uniquely determine the ratio $a_{00}^4 : a_{10}^4 : a_{20}^4 : a_{01}^4 : a_{11}^4$, which just coincides with the list for the case $m = 4$, substituted by $s_0 = 1$ (remark that $a_{30}^4 = 0$). This also gives a generator of $(p\Lambda_1 + q\Lambda_2) \otimes V_{n-2q-6}$ in $\mathcal{LH}_n^+$.

In case $s_0 = 0$ the situation is completely different. In this case we have $a_{ij}^4 = 0$ for $i + j \geq 2$. Hence, among the above six equations on a_{ij}^4 the first equation only remains. The ratio of three non-zero coefficients a_{00}^4, a_{10}^4, a_{01}^4 is not uniquely determined by this single equation. But from the list for the case $m = 4$ we have

$$
\begin{aligned}
a_{00}^4 &= \frac{1}{6}(d + 2q - 2)(d + p + 2q)(d + p + 2q + 1)(d + p + 2q + 2) \\
&\quad + (d + p + 2q)(d + 2p + 2q) \\
&= \frac{1}{6}(d + p + 2q - 1)(d + p + 2q)\{(d + 2q + 2)(d + p + 2q) - 4(p - 1)\}, \\
a_{10}^4 &= -(d + 2q - 2)(d + p + 2q + 1)(d + p + 2q + 2) - 4p(d + p + 2q) \\
&\quad - 2(d + 2p + 2q + 2) \\
&= -(d + 2q + 2)(d + p + 2q - 1)(d + p + 2q), \\
a_{01}^4 &= 2(d + p + 2q - 1)(d + p + 2q),
\end{aligned}
$$

after substituting $s_0 = 0$. Thus, dividing by $(d + p + 2q - 1)(d + p + 2q)$, we may consider that

$$
\begin{aligned}
a_{00}^4 &= (d + 2q + 2)(d + p + 2q) - 4(p - 1), \\
a_{10}^4 &= -6(d + 2q + 2), \\
a_{01}^4 &= 12
\end{aligned}
$$

gives a generator of $(p\Lambda_1 + q\Lambda_2) \otimes V_{n-2q-6}$ in $\mathcal{LH}_n^+$. To obtain a generator of $(p\Lambda_1 + q\Lambda_2) \otimes V_{n-2q-6}$ in $\mathcal{LH}_n^-$, we must carry out a similar procedure which we explained in the case $m = 3$, $s_0 = 0$.

For example, we consider the case $n = 5$, $p = 3$ and $q = 0$. In this case we have

$$\mathcal{LH}_5^+ \supset (3\Lambda_1) \otimes (V_5 + V_3 + V_1 + V_{-1}),$$
$$\mathcal{LH}_5^- \supset (3\Lambda_1) \otimes (V_1 + V_{-1} + V_{-3} + V_{-5}).$$

We are now considering generators of the component $(3\Lambda_1) \otimes V_{-1}$ in $\mathcal{LH}_5 = \mathcal{LH}_5^+ \oplus \mathcal{LH}_5^-$. A generator of $(3\Lambda_1) \otimes V_{-1}$ in $\mathcal{LH}_5^+$ is given by

$$f_+ = a_{00}^4 \, F[1,0,0,0,3,0] + a_{10}^4 \, F[0,1,0,1,2,0] + a_{01}^4 \, F[0,0,1,2,1,0]$$

with

$$a_{00}^4 = (d+2)(d+3) - 8, \quad a_{10}^4 = -6(d+2), \quad a_{01}^4 = 12,$$

as stated before. Next, we must find a generator of $(3\Lambda_1) \otimes V_{-1}$ in $\mathcal{LH}_5^-$. For this purpose we have only to find a generator of $(3\Lambda_1) \otimes V_1$ in $\mathcal{LH}_5^+$ and exchange z and w in it. But this is the third component, and we have already known its explicit form:

$$a_{00}^3 \, F[1,0,0,1,2,0] + a_{10}^3 \, F[0,1,0,2,1,0] + a_{01}^3 \, F[0,0,1,3,0,0]$$

with

$$a_{00}^3 = d^2 + 3d - 6, \quad a_{10}^3 = -4d, \quad a_{01}^3 = 4.$$

Thus the polynomial

$$f_- = a_{01}^3 \, F[1,0,0,0,3,0] + a_{10}^3 \, F[0,1,0,1,2,0] + a_{00}^3 \, F[0,0,1,2,1,0]$$

generates the space $(3\Lambda_1) \otimes V_{-1}$ in $\mathcal{LH}_5^-$. It is easy to see that f_+ and f_- are linearly independent since $d \geq 4$. (Compare the list in [p.102; 10].)

The expression of a_{ij}^m in Conjecture 4.1 is completely different from a conjecture given in [p.108$\sim$; 11]. To show the equivalence of these two conjectures, we must prove several identities such as

$$\sum_{\tau=0}^{l} \frac{(2l)!}{2^\tau \, \tau! \, (2l - 2\tau)!} \prod_{v=\tau+1}^{l} (d + 2q + 2v - 4) = \prod_{v=1}^{l} (d + 2q + 2l + 2v - 5).$$

To show the equivalence is our another subject. The above identity appears when we compare two coefficients of a_{00}^{2l+1} in two conjectures. It is a coefficient of s_0^{2l} in a_{00}^{2l+1}, which is the highest term of s_0 in a_{00}^{2l+1}.

We cannot yet complete the proof of Conjecture 4.1. It is our principal subject in future investigations.

5. Some Examples of Reproducing Kernels of Principal Components

In this section we give the reproducing kernels of the principal part of irreducible subspaces of P_n on some orbits in some cases. The generator of the principal irreducible component $(p\Lambda_1 + q\Lambda_2) \otimes V_k \subset P_n$ with $p + 2q = n$ $(p \geq 0, q \geq 0)$, $|k| \leq p$ and $k \equiv p \pmod 2$ is given by

$$(z \cdot \alpha)^{(p+k)/2} (w \cdot \alpha)^{(p-k)/2} \{(z \cdot \alpha)(w \cdot \beta) - (z \cdot \beta)(w \cdot \alpha)\}^q$$

with $\alpha^2 = \alpha \cdot \beta = \beta^2 = 0$, as stated before.

The dimension of the $K_{\mathbf{R}}$-irreducible component $(p\Lambda_1+q\Lambda_2)\otimes V_k$ can be calculated by the formula

$$\frac{1}{(d-2)!(d-4)!} (p+1)(d+2q-4)(d+p+2q-3)$$

$$\times (d+2p+2q-2) \cdot \prod_{l=1}^{d-5} (q+l) \cdot \prod_{l=1}^{d-5} (p+q+l+1).$$

For details see [10], [11].

In the following we denote by dh the Haar measure on $SO(d)$, and we put $e_j = {}^t(0\cdots 0 \overset{j}{1} 0\cdots 0)$. For $\widetilde{X} = \begin{pmatrix} 0 & X \\ {}^tX & 0 \end{pmatrix} \in \mathfrak{p}$, $X = (x\ y)$ and $g = \mathrm{Ad}\begin{pmatrix} A & 0 \\ 0 & R(\theta) \end{pmatrix} \in K_{\mathbf{R}}$ $(A \in SO(d))$ with $R(\theta) = \begin{pmatrix} \cos\theta & -\sin\theta \\ \sin\theta & \cos\theta \end{pmatrix}$, we have

$$\Psi(g\widetilde{X}) = \begin{pmatrix} e^{-i\theta}Az \\ e^{i\theta}Aw \end{pmatrix}.$$

For a polynomial f on $\mathfrak{p}$ it is valid that

$$\int_{K_{\mathbf{R}}} f(g\widetilde{X}_0)dg = \frac{1}{2\pi} \int_0^{2\pi} \int_{SO(d)} f \circ \Psi^{-1}\left(\begin{pmatrix} e^{-i\theta}hz_0 \\ e^{i\theta}hw_0 \end{pmatrix} \right) dhd\theta,$$

where $\widetilde{X}_0 = \Psi^{-1}\left(\begin{pmatrix} z_0 \\ w_0 \end{pmatrix} \right) \in \mathfrak{p}$.

We put

$$\widetilde{E}_0 = \Psi^{-1}\left(\begin{pmatrix} e_1+ie_2 \\ e_3+ie_4 \end{pmatrix} \right), \quad \widetilde{E}_1 = \Psi^{-1}\left(\begin{pmatrix} e_1+ie_2 \\ e_1+ie_2 \end{pmatrix} \right).$$

For $f \in \mathcal{H}_n$ we denote by $\langle f \rangle$ the subspace generated by the set $\{f(gX)\,;\,g \in K_{\mathbf{R}}\}$. Let $\widetilde{X} = \Psi^{-1}\left(\begin{pmatrix} z \\ w \end{pmatrix} \right)$, $\widetilde{X}' = \Psi^{-1}\left(\begin{pmatrix} z' \\ w' \end{pmatrix} \right) \in \mathfrak{p}$.

We need the following formulas for our calculations.

Proposition 5.1 (cf. [2], [4], [12]). *We put $e_0 = e_1 + ie_2$ and $P_{n,d}(t)$ denotes the Legendre polynomials of degree n and dimension d.*

(1) For z, $w \in \mathbf{C}^d\backslash\{0\}$ the following formula is valid.

$$\int_{SO(d)} (he_0 \cdot z)^n \overline{(he_0 \cdot w)^m}dh = \delta_{n,m}2^n \lambda_{n,d}(z^2)^{n/2}(\overline{w}^2)^{n/2}P_{n,p}\left(\frac{z \cdot \overline{w}}{(z^2)^{1/2}(\overline{w}^2)^{1/2}} \right),$$

where $\lambda_{n,d} = \dfrac{n!\Gamma(d/2)}{2^n\Gamma(n+d/2)}$.

(2) For any harmonic polynomial f_n on $\mathbf{C}^d$ with degree n and any $z \in \mathbf{C}^d$, it is valid that

$$2^n \delta_{n,m}f_n(z) = \dim H_n(\mathbf{C}^d) \int_{SO(d)} f_n(he_0)\overline{(he_0 \cdot \overline{z})^m}dh,$$

where $H_n(\mathbf{C}^d)$ is the space of homogeneous harmonic polynomials of degree n in dimension d.

Suppose $\widetilde{X}_0 \in \mathfrak{p} \backslash \{0\}$, V is a $K_{\mathbf{R}}$-irreducible subspace of $\mathcal{H}_n$. Let $K(\widetilde{X}, \widetilde{Y})$ be the function on $\mathfrak{p} \times \mathfrak{p}$ which satisfies the following conditions:

$$K(\ , g\widetilde{X}_0) \in V \qquad (g \in K_{\mathbf{R}}), \tag{5.1}$$

$$K(\widetilde{X}, \widetilde{X}') = \overline{K(\widetilde{X}', \widetilde{X})} \qquad (\widetilde{X}, \widetilde{X}' \in \mathfrak{p}), \tag{5.2}$$

$$K(\widetilde{X}, \widetilde{X}') = K(g\widetilde{X}, g\widetilde{X}') \qquad (g \in K_{\mathbf{R}}), \tag{5.3}$$

$$\int_{K_{\mathbf{R}}} f(g\widetilde{X}_0) K(\widetilde{X}, g\widetilde{X}_0) dg = f(\widetilde{X}) \qquad (f \in V). \tag{5.4}$$

We put for $\widetilde{X}, \widetilde{Y} \in \mathfrak{p}$

$$H(\widetilde{X}, \widetilde{Y}) = \int_{K_{\mathbf{R}}} K(\widetilde{X}, g\widetilde{X}_0) K(g\widetilde{X}_0, \widetilde{Y}) dg.$$

Then $H(\widetilde{X}, \widetilde{Y})$ is the reproducing kernel in V on the orbit $K_{\mathbf{R}} \widetilde{X}_0$, i.e., for any $f \in V$

$$H(\ , Y) \in V \qquad (Y \in \mathfrak{p}),$$

$$H(\widetilde{X}, \widetilde{X}') = \overline{H(\widetilde{X}', \widetilde{X})} \qquad (\widetilde{X}, \widetilde{X}' \in \mathfrak{p}),$$

$$H(\widetilde{X}, \widetilde{X}') = H(g\widetilde{X}, g\widetilde{X}') \qquad (g \in K_{\mathbf{R}}),$$

$$\int_{K_{\mathbf{R}}} f(g\widetilde{X}_0) H(\widetilde{X}, g\widetilde{X}_0) dg = f(\widetilde{X}).$$

Furthermore we have for any $g \in K_{\mathbf{R}}$

$$K(\widetilde{X}, g\widetilde{X}_0) = H(\widetilde{X}, g\widetilde{X}_0).$$

(Note that the right hand side of the equality (7.4) in our previous paper [p.118; 11] should be replaced by " $= f(\widetilde{X})$ $(f \in V)$", as in (5.4) stated above. The equality in [p.119; 11] line 6 from the top should be similarly replaced.)

Next we show some examples of reproducing kernels of irreducible subspaces of P_n.

Example 5.1. In the following we assume $\alpha^2 = \alpha \cdot \beta = \beta^2 = 0$. We put

$$P_{n,p,k,q} = \langle (z \cdot \alpha)^{\frac{p+k}{2}} (w \cdot \alpha)^{\frac{p-k}{2}} \{ (z \cdot \alpha)(w \cdot \beta) - (z \cdot \beta)(w \cdot \alpha) \}^q \rangle \subset P_n,$$

where $p + 2q = n$ $(p \geq 0, q \geq 0)$, $|k| \leq p$ and $k \equiv p \pmod 2$. Note that this space corresponds to $(p\Lambda_1 + q\Lambda_2) \otimes V_k$.

(1) Let $p = n, q = 0, |k| \leq p, k \equiv p \pmod 2$ and

$$P_{n,n,k,0} = \langle (z \cdot \alpha)^{\frac{n+k}{2}} (w \cdot \alpha)^{\frac{n-k}{2}} \rangle.$$

We define

$$K_{n,n,k,0}(\widetilde{X}, \widetilde{X}') = \frac{1}{2^n} \dim P_{n,n,k,0} \, (z \cdot \overline{z}')^{\frac{n+k}{2}} (w \cdot \overline{w}')^{\frac{n-k}{2}}.$$

Then we can see that $K_{n,n,k,0}$ satisfies (5.1)$\sim$(5.4) for $\widetilde{X}_0 = \widetilde{E}_1$. Therefore the reproducing kernel in $P_{n,n,k,0}$ on the orbit $K_{\mathbf{R}}\widetilde{E}_1$ is

$$H_{n,n,k,0}(\widetilde{X}, \widetilde{Y}) = \int_{K_{\mathbf{R}}} K_{n,n,k,0}(\widetilde{X}, g\widetilde{E}_1) K_{n,n,k,0}(g\widetilde{E}_1, \widetilde{Y}) dg.$$

(2) Let $p = k = n - 2, q = 1$ and

$$P_{n,n-2,n-2,1} = \langle (z \cdot \alpha)^{n-2} \{ (z \cdot \alpha)(w \cdot \beta) - (z \cdot \beta)(w \cdot \alpha) \} \rangle,$$

and we define

$$K_{n,n-2,n-2,1}(\widetilde{X}, \widetilde{X}') = \frac{1}{2^n} \dim P_{n,n-2,n-2,1} \, (z \cdot \overline{z}')^{n-2} \{ (z \cdot \overline{z}')(w \cdot \overline{w}') - (z \cdot \overline{w}')(w \cdot \overline{z}') \}.$$

Then we can see that $K_{n,n-2,n-2,1}$ satisfies (5.1)$\sim$(5.4) for $\widetilde{X}_0 = \widetilde{E}_0$. Therefore the reproducing kernel in $P_{n,n-2,n-2,1}$ on the orbit $K_{\mathbf{R}}\widetilde{E}_0$ is

$$H_{n,n-2,n-2,1}(\widetilde{X}, \widetilde{Y}) = \int_{K_{\mathbf{R}}} K_{n,n-2,n-2,1}(\widetilde{X}, g\widetilde{E}_0) K_{n,n-2,n-2,1}(g\widetilde{E}_0, \widetilde{Y}) dg.$$

(3) Let $p = n - 2, k = 2 - n, q = 1$ and

$$P_{n,n-2,2-n,1} = \langle (w \cdot \alpha)^{n-2} \{ (z \cdot \alpha)(w \cdot \beta) - (z \cdot \beta)(w \cdot \alpha) \} \rangle,$$

and we define

$$K_{n,n-2,2-n,1}(\widetilde{X}, \widetilde{X}') = \frac{1}{2^n} \dim P_{n,n-2,2-n,1} \, (w \cdot \overline{w}')^{n-2} \{ (z \cdot \overline{z}')(w \cdot \overline{w}') - (z \cdot \overline{w}')(w \cdot \overline{z}') \}.$$

Then we can see that $K_{n,n-2,2-n,1}$ satisfies (5.1)$\sim$(5.4) for $\widetilde{X}_0 = \widetilde{E}_0$. Therefore the reproducing kernel in $P_{n,n-2,2-n,1}$ on the orbit $K_{\mathbf{R}}\widetilde{E}_0$ is

$$H_{n,n-2,2-n,1}(\widetilde{X}, \widetilde{Y}) = \int_{K_{\mathbf{R}}} K_{n,n-2,2-n,1}(\widetilde{X}, g\widetilde{E}_0) K_{n,n-2,2-n,1}(g\widetilde{E}_0, \widetilde{Y}) dg.$$

References

[1] S. Helgason, *Groups and Geometric Analysis*, Academic Press Inc., Orlando, 1984.

[2] K. Ii, On a Bargmann-type transform and a Hilbert space of holomorphic functions, *Tôhoku Math. J.*, **38** (1986), 57–69.

[3] B. Kostant and S. Rallis, Orbits and representations associated with symmetric spaces, *Amer. J. Math.*, **93** (1971), 753–809.

[4] C. Müller, Spherical Harmonics, *Lecture Notes in Math.*, **17** (1966), Springer-Verlag.

[5] M. Takeuchi, *Modern Spherical Functions*, Translations of Mathematical Monographs vol.**135**, Amer. Math. Soc., 1994.

[6] R. Wada, Explicit formulas for the reproducing kernels of the space of harmonic polynomials in the case of classical real rank 1, *Scientiae Mathematicae Japonicae*, **65** (2007), 384–406.

[7] R. Wada and Y. Agaoka, The reproducing kernels of the space of harmonic polynomials in the case of real rank 1, in *Microlocal Analysis and Complex Fourier Analysis* (Ed. T. Kawai, K. Fujita), 297–316, World Scientific, New Jersey (2002).

[8] R. Wada and Y. Agaoka, Some properties of harmonic polynomials in the case of $\mathfrak{so}(p, 2)$, in *Legal Informatics, Economic Science and Mathematical Research* (Ed. M. Kitahara, C. Czerkawski), 81–88, Kyushu University Press, (2014).

[9] R. Wada and Y. Agaoka, On some properties of harmonic polynomials in the case of $\mathfrak{so}(p, 2)$: Irreducible decomposition and integral formulas, in *New Solutions in Legal Informatics, Economic Sciences and Mathematics* (Ed. M. Kitahara, K. Okamura), 123–142, Kyushu University Press, (2015).

[10] R. Wada and Y. Agaoka, Explicit irreducible decomposition of harmonic polynomials in the case of $\mathfrak{so}(p, 2)$, in *Contemporary Works in Economic Sciences* (Ed. M. Kitahara, H. Teramoto), 83–109, Kyushu University Press, (2016).

[11] R. Wada and Y. Agaoka, Generators of irreducible components of harmonic polynomials in the case of $\mathfrak{so}(d, 2)$, in *Challenging Researches in Economic Sciences* (Ed. M. Kitahara, H. Teramoto), 93–124, Kyushu University Press, (2017).

[12] R. Wada and M. Morimoto, A uniqueness set for the differential operator $\Delta_z + \lambda^2$, *Tokyo J. Math.*, **10** (1987), 93–105.

Chapter 5

A Study on Selecting an Oblique Coordinate System for Rotation-Invariant Blend Crossover in a Real-Coded Genetic Algorithm

Setsuko Sakai and Tetsuyuki Takahama**

Faculty of Commercial Sciences, Hiroshima Shudo University
1-1 Ozuka-Higashi 1-chome, Asaminami-ku, Hiroshima, JAPAN 731-3195
**Graduate School of Information Sciences, Hiroshima City University*
4-1 Ozuka-Higashi 3-chome, Asaminami-ku, Hiroshima, JAPAN 731-3194

Abstract

A representative crossover in real-coded genetic algorithms is blend crossover (BLX-α). The blend crossover, which is two-parent crossover, has been applied to many applications because it can be implemented easily. Also, it can realize excellent diversity because a child is generated in an extended region including two parents. However, since the child is generated for each variable independently, the performance deteriorates in a problem with strong dependency among variables. In this study, we propose an oblique crossover (OBX) where an oblique coordinate system is built from difference vectors among individuals and a blend crossover along the oblique coordinate system is performed. The oblique crossover is rotation-invariant because when the distribution of individuals is rotated, the oblique coordinate system is rotated and a child is generated according to the rotated coordinate system. However, the diversity tends to be lost because the child is generated in narrow area compared with BLX-α. In this research, we study how to select a proper oblique coordinate system from difference vectors in order to improve the diversity. The effect of selecting an oblique coordinate system is shown by solving thirteen benchmark problems.

Key Words:

Rotation-invariant crossover, Blend crossover, Oblique coordinate system, Real-coded genetic algorithm, Evolutionary algorithms

1. Introduction

There exist many studies on solving optimization problems using evolutionary algorithms (EAs), which are inspired by biological evolution, such as genetic algorithm [1], evolution strategy and differential evolution [2, 3]. In EAs, a population or multiple search points are used to search for an optimal solution. In general, EAs are stochastic direct search methods, which only need function values to be optimized, and are easy to implement. For this reason, EAs have been successfully applied to various optimization problems including non-linear, non-differentiable, non-convex and multimodal functions [4–6].

In EAs, various genetic operations including crossover and mutation have been proposed. The crossover is used to generate a child from parent individuals and the mutation is used to perturb the child. In this study, the crossover for real-coded genetic algorithms is paid attention to. A representative crossover in real-coded genetic algorithms is blend crossover (BLX-α). The blend crossover, which is two-parent crossover, has been applied to many applications because it can be implemented easily. Also, it can realize excellent diversity because a child is generated in an extended region including two parents. However, the performance of BLX-α deteriorates in problems with strong dependency among decision variables, where variables are related strongly each other. One of the desirable properties of optimization algorithms for solving the problems with strong dependency is rotation-invariant property. The rotation-invariant algorithms can solve rotated problems where variables are strongly related as in the same way of solving non-rotated problems.

Table 1 shows various crossover operations and their features. Two-parent crossover operations such as BLX-α (Blend Crossover) [7] and SBX (Simulated Binary Crossover) [8] create a child by generating each element or gene of the child independently according to a uniform distribution and a polynomial distribution, respectively. Therefore, the operations are not rotation-invariant. It is difficult for these operations to solve problems with strong dependency among variables. There are some rotation-invariant two-parent crossovers where an orthogonal coordinate system is built using a population and children are generated using the coordinate system: RIX (Rotation-Invariant Crossover) [9] generates a set of vectors from the centroid of a population to each individual in the population, and an orthogonal coordinate system is built by randomly selected vectors from the set using Gram-Schmidt orthonormalization. EIG (Eigen vector-based crossover) [10] obtains eigen vectors from the variance-covariance matrix of all individuals in a population and the eigen vectors are used as an orthogonal coordinate system. These crossover operations are rotation-invariant, because the orthogonal coordinate system rotates according to the rotation of the individuals. In multi-parent crossover operations such as SPX (Simplex Crossover) [11] and REX (Real-Coded Ensemble Crossover) [12], parents are selected from a population, and children are generated using vectors from the centroid of the parents to each parent according to a uniform distribution or a normal distribution. The crossover operations use an oblique coordinate system, because the vectors are not orthogonal. Also, the crossover operations are rotation-invariant, because the oblique coordinate system rotates according to the rotation of the parents. However, it is difficult to keep diversity and to search outside of the population because children tend to be generated near the center of parents.

Table 1. Crossover operations for real-coded genetic algorithms

Crossover	Parents	Coordinate system	Rotation-invariant
BLX-α, SBX	Two	Cartesian coordinate system	No
RIX, EIG	Two	Orthogonal coordinate system generated from individuals	Yes
SPX, REX	Multiple	Oblique coordinate system generated from individuals	Yes
OBX	Two	Oblique coordinate system generated from individuals	Yes

In this study, OBX (Oblique Crossover), which is new two-parent crossover using an oblique coordinate system, is proposed. The oblique coordinate system is built from difference vectors among individuals. OBX employs the method of generating a child similar to BLX-α based on the oblique coordinate system. OBX is rotation-invariant, because the oblique coordinate system rotates according to the rotation of the individuals and a child is generated according to the rotated coordinate system. However, the diversity tends to be lost because the child is generated in narrow area compared with BLX-α. In this research, we study how to select a proper oblique coordinate system from difference vectors in order to improve the diversity.

The effect of selecting an oblique coordinate system is shown by solving thirteen benchmark problems.

In Section 2, related works are described. GA is briefly explained in Section 3. In Section 4, OBX is proposed. The experimental results are shown in Section 5. Finally, conclusions are described in Section 6.

2. Related Works

2.1 Two-parent crossover

In two-parent crossover, two parents $\boldsymbol{p} = (p_j)$ and $\boldsymbol{q} = (q_j)$ are selected from a population and a child is generated by the crossover. BLX-α is explained as representative two-parent crossover.

BLX-α is a crossover operation which generates a child $\boldsymbol{x}' = (x'_j)$ in an extended hyper-rectangle formed by two parents as follows:

$$x'_j = r_j p_j + (1 - r_j) q_j \tag{1}$$

where r_i is a uniform random number in $[-\alpha, 1 + \alpha]$ and generated in each dimension independently. The parameter α ($\alpha \geq 0$) specifies how much the region, in which a child will be generated, is enlarged. If α is zero, the child is generated in a hyper-rectangle that is formed by two parents. Therefore, the blend crossover is not rotation-invariant. An example of the rectangle is shown in Figure 1 by dotted lines.

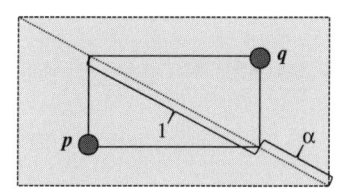

Figure 1. Area of children generated by BLX-α

2.2 Multi-parent crossover

There exist some crossover operations using multiple (more than two) parents such as UNDX (Unimodal Normal Distribution Crossover) [13], SPX (Simplex Crossover) [14] and REX (Real-Coded Ensemble Crossover) [15]. REX is explained as representative multi-parent crossover.

REX is rotation-invariant and scale-invariant crossover. REX generates a child from multiple parents randomly selected from a population without overlapping each other. Let parents be denoted by $\{\boldsymbol{x}^1, \boldsymbol{x}^2, \cdots, \boldsymbol{x}^m\}$ and their centroid by $\boldsymbol{x}^g$. The child $\boldsymbol{x}'$ is generated according to the following equations:

$$\boldsymbol{x}' = \boldsymbol{x}^g + \sum_{i=1}^{m} \xi^i (\boldsymbol{x}^i - \boldsymbol{x}^g) \tag{2}$$

$$\xi^i \;\sim\; \phi(0,\sigma_\xi^2),\; \sigma_\xi^2 = \frac{1}{m} \tag{3}$$

$$\boldsymbol{x}^g \;=\; \frac{1}{m}\sum_{i=1}^{m}\boldsymbol{x}^i \tag{4}$$

where m is the number of parents $(m \geq D)$, ξ^i is a random number for each parent obeying $\phi(\cdot)$, and $\phi(0,\sigma_\xi^2)$ is a symmetric probability distribution with mean 0 and variance σ_ξ^2. Examples of ϕ are as follows:

$$\phi(0,\sigma^2) \;=\; N(0,(\sqrt{1/m}\,)^2) \tag{5}$$
$$\phi(0,\sigma^2) \;=\; U(-\sqrt{3/m},\sqrt{3/m}\,) \tag{6}$$

where N is a normal distribution and $U(l,r)$ is a uniform distribution in $[l,r]$.

Figure 2 shows an example of children generated by REX using the uniform distribution in two-dimensions where $D = 2$ and $m = 3$.

Figure 2. An example of children generated by REX

3.   Optimization by Genetic Algorithm

3.1   Optimization problems

In this study, the following optimization problem with lower bound and upper bound constraints will be discussed.

$$\begin{aligned}
\text{minimize} \quad & f(\boldsymbol{x}) \\
\text{subject to} \quad & l_i \leq x_i \leq u_i,\; i = 1,\ldots,D,
\end{aligned} \tag{7}$$

where $\boldsymbol{x} = (x_1, x_2, \cdots, x_D)$ is a D dimensional vector and $f(\boldsymbol{x})$ is an objective function. The function f is a nonlinear real-valued function. Values l_i and u_i are the lower bound and the upper bound of x_i, respectively. Let the search space in which every point satisfies the lower and upper bound constraints be denoted by $\mathfrak{S}$.

3.2   Genetic algorithm

Genetic algorithm (GA) is a stochastic multi-point search method, which models the process of biological evolution, and has been applied to various application areas [1].

The algorithm of GA is as follows:

1. Initialization: An initial population is created randomly, where each gene x_i^k of an individual $\boldsymbol{x}^k$ is created as a uniform random number in the interval $[l_i, u_i]$.

2. Stopping condition: The algorithm will stop when some conditions are satisfied. For example, it stops when the number of function evaluations reaches the predefined maximum number of function evaluations.

3. Parent selection: Parents who will generate children are selected from the population according to some predefined method.

4. Crossover: Parents are mated usually with predefined probability called crossover rate, and their children are generated.

5. Mutation: Children are mutated by a mutation operation such as uniform mutation and Gaussian mutation.

6. Survivor selection: The population in the next generation is formed by a set of individuals selected from the union of the current population and the generated children. Go back to 2.

In this study, following GA is adopted: As for parent selection, each invididual is selected as one of two parents for crossover. Crossover rate is 1. Mutation is not applied. As for survivor selection, the better individial between the parent and the child survives in the next generation. It is thought that the parent selection and the survivor selection is same as differential evolution.

Figure 3 shows the pseudo-code of GA in this study, where t is the number of generations, FE is the number of function evalutions and FE_{max} is the maximum number of function evaluations.

```
GA()
{
// Initialize a population
  P=N individuals generated randomly in 𝕲;
  FE=FE+N;
  for(t=1;  FE < FEmax;  t++) {
    for(i=1;  i ≤ N;  i++) {
        xʳ=randomly selected from P s.t. r≠i.
        x'=generated from xⁱ and xʳ by crossover;
        FE=FE+1;
// Survivor selection
        if(f(x') < f(xⁱ))  zⁱ = x';
        else zⁱ = xⁱ;
    }
    P = {zⁱ};
  }
}
```

Figure 3. The pseudo-code of a real-coded GA

4. Proposed Method

In this study, a child x' is generated from parents p and q in the population $P = \{x^i \mid i = 1, 2, \cdots, N\}$ same as BLX-α.

4.1 Oblique crossover (OBX)

In two parents, let p and q regard a starting position and a goal position, respectively. The axis vectors for an oblique coordinate system can be obtained as follows:

1. Let current position $p_0 = p$. k=1.

2. The difference vector from the current position to the goal position $d_k = q - p_{k-1}$ is obtained.

3. An axis vector v_k for the oblique coordinate system is generated from the population P where v_k is a difference vector between arbitrary two individuals.

4. The orthogonal projection e_k of d_k onto v_k is obtained. By moving from the current position toward the direction of the projection, the position can approach the goal position. The projection corresponds to a kind of unit vector of the axis.

$$
\begin{aligned}
e_k &= ||d_k|| \cos\theta \frac{v_k}{||v_k||} = \frac{(d_k, v_k)}{||v_k||} \frac{v_k}{||v_k||} \\
&= \frac{(d_k, v_k)}{(v_k, v_k)} v_k \\
p_k &= p_{k-1} + e_k
\end{aligned}
\tag{8}
$$

where θ is the angle between d_k and v_k.

5. If $k < n - 1$, $k=k + 1$ and go back to 2.

6. If $k = n - 1$, $e_n = q - p_{n-1}$.

Therefore, the following equation is satisfied:

$$
q = p + \sum_{k=1}^{n} e_k
\tag{9}
$$

Figure 4 shows an example of the oblique coordinate system for OBX in 3 dimensions.

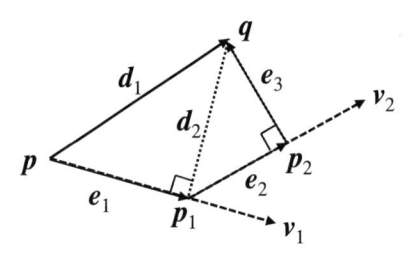

Figure 4. Oblique coordinate system

A child x' is generated according to the obtained oblique coordinate system $\{e_k|k = 1, 2, \cdots, n\}$ as follows:

$$
x' = p + \sum_{k=1}^{n} r_k e_k
\tag{10}
$$

where r_k is a uniform random number for each axis vector and is generated in $[-\alpha, 1 + \alpha]$ same as BLX-α. Figure 5 shows an example of area for generating children in 2 dimensions.

4.2   Another oblique crossover (OBX2)

In OBX, $n - 1$ vectors $E_1 = \{e_k|k = 1, 2, \cdots, n - 1\}$ are obtained according to Eq. (8), and a vector e_n is not obtained according to Eq. (8) but $e_n = q - p_{n-1}$ in order to satisfy Eq. (9).

On the contrary, it is possible to generate all axis vectors $E_2 = \{e_k|k = 1, 2, \cdots, n\}$ according to Eq. (8).

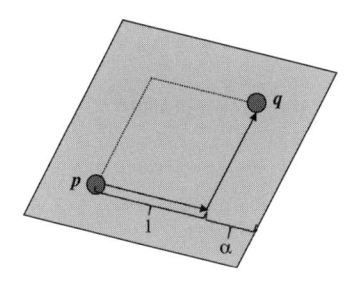

Figure 5. Area in which children are generated by OBX

In another oblique crossover called OBX2, a child is generated according to Eq. (10) using the oblique coordinate system E_2. OBX2 does not satisfy Eq. (9). However, it is thought that OBX2 can increase diversity of children compared with OBX.

OBX2 can be realized by replacing step 5 with the following and by deleting step 6 in OBX algorithm.

5. If $k < n$, $k=k+1$ and go back to 2.

4.3 Rotation-invariant

If R is a rotation matrix, $R^T R = I$ is satisfied. The inner product is invariant before rotation and after rotation as follows:

$$
\begin{aligned}
(R\boldsymbol{x}, R\boldsymbol{y}) &= (R\boldsymbol{x})^T (R\boldsymbol{y}) = \boldsymbol{x}^T R^T R \boldsymbol{y} = \boldsymbol{x}^T \boldsymbol{y} \\
&= (\boldsymbol{x}, \boldsymbol{y})
\end{aligned}
\tag{11}
$$

In the algorithm above, the addition and the subtraction between two vectors are rotation-invariant. An inner product $\frac{(\boldsymbol{d}_k, \boldsymbol{v}_k)}{(\boldsymbol{v}_k, \boldsymbol{v}_k)}$ used by scalar multiplication is not changed before and after rotation. Therefore, the algorithm can realize rotation-invariant crossover.

5. Numerical Experiments

In this paper, well-known thirteen benchmark problems are solved.

5.1 Test problems

The 13 scalable benchmark functions are shown in Table 2 [16]. Every function has an optimal objective value 0. Some characteristics are briefly summarized as follows: Functions f_1 to f_4 are continuous unimodal functions. The function f_5 is Rosenbrock function which is unimodal for 2- and 3-dimensions but may have multiple minima in high dimension cases [17]. The function f_6 is a discontinuous step function, and f_7 is a noisy quartic function. Functions f_8 to f_{13} are multimodal functions and the number of their local minima increases exponentially with the problem dimension [18].

5.2 Conditions of experiments

Experimental conditions for GA are as follows: Population size $N = 100$. The value of α for BLX is 0.5, α for OBX and OBX2 is taken from 0.5, 0.6 and 0.7 to keep diversity.

Independent 50 runs are performed for 13 problems. The number of dimensions for the problems is 30 (D=30). Each run stops when the number of function evaluations (FEs) exceeds the maximum number of evaluations $FE_{\max}$. In each function, different $FE_{\max}$ is adopted.

Table 2. Test functions of dimension D. These are sphere, Schwefel 2.22, Schwefel 1.2, Schwefel 2.21, Rosenbrock, step, noisy quartic, Schwefel 2.26, Rastrigin, Ackley, Griewank, and two penalized functions, respectively [19]

Test functions	Bound constraints
$f_1(\boldsymbol{x}) = \sum_{i=1}^{D} x_i^2$	$[-100, 100]^D$
$f_2(\boldsymbol{x}) = \sum_{i=1}^{D} |x_i| + \prod_{i=1}^{D} |x_i|$	$[-10, 10]^D$
$f_3(\boldsymbol{x}) = \sum_{i=1}^{D} \left(\sum_{j=1}^{i} x_j \right)^2$	$[-100, 100]^D$
$f_4(\boldsymbol{x}) = \max_i \{|x_i|\}$	$[-100, 100]^D$
$f_5(\boldsymbol{x}) = \sum_{i=1}^{D-1} \left[100(x_{i+1} - x_i^2)^2 + (x_i - 1)^2 \right]$	$[-30, 30]^D$
$f_6(\boldsymbol{x}) = \sum_{i=1}^{D} \lfloor x_i + 0.5 \rfloor^2$	$[-100, 100]^D$
$f_7(\boldsymbol{x}) = \sum_{i=1}^{D} i x_i^4 + rand[0, 1)$	$[-1.28, 1.28]^D$
$f_8(\boldsymbol{x}) = \sum_{i=1}^{D} -x_i \sin \sqrt{|x_i|} + D \cdot 418.98288727243369$	$[-500, 500]^D$
$f_9(\boldsymbol{x}) = \sum_{i=1}^{D} \left[x_i^2 - 10 \cos(2\pi x_i) + 10 \right]$	$[-5.12, 5.12]^D$
$f_{10}(\boldsymbol{x}) = -20 \exp \left(-0.2 \sqrt{\frac{1}{D} \sum_{i=1}^{D} x_i^2} \right) - \exp \left(\frac{1}{D} \sum_{i=1}^{D} \cos(2\pi x_i) \right) + 20$ $+ e$	$[-32, 32]^D$
$f_{11}(\boldsymbol{x}) = \frac{1}{4000} \sum_{i=1}^{D} x_i^2 - \prod_{i=1}^{D} \cos \left(\frac{x_i}{\sqrt{i}} \right) + 1$	$[-600, 600]^D$
$f_{12}(\boldsymbol{x}) = \frac{\pi}{D} [10 \sin^2(\pi y_1) + \sum_{i=1}^{D-1} (y_i - 1)^2 \{1 + 10 \sin^2(\pi y_{i+1})\}$ $+ (y_D - 1)^2] + \sum_{i=1}^{D} u(x_i, 10, 100, 4)$ where $y_i = 1 + \frac{1}{4}(x_i + 1)$ and $u(x_i, a, k, m) = \begin{cases} k(x_i - a)^m & x_i > a \\ 0 & -a \le x_i \le a \\ k(-x_i - a)^m & x_i < -a \end{cases}$	$[-50, 50]^D$
$f_{13}(\boldsymbol{x}) = 0.1[\sin^2(3\pi x_1) + \sum_{i=1}^{D-1} (x_i - 1)^2 \{1 + \sin^2(3\pi x_{i+1})\}$ $+ (x_D - 1)^2 \{1 + \sin^2(2\pi x_D)\}] + \sum_{i=1}^{D} u(x_i, 5, 100, 4)$	$[-50, 50]^D$

5.3 Rotated problems

In order to investigate the performance for non-separable problems, the benchmark problems are rotated: A candidate solution z is converted as $x = Mz$ and $f(x)$ is minimized, where M is a rotation matrix. In this study, Helmert matrix Eq. (12) is used as the rotation matrix.

$$
M = \begin{pmatrix}
\frac{1}{\sqrt{D}} & \frac{1}{\sqrt{D}} & \frac{1}{\sqrt{D}} & \cdots & \frac{1}{\sqrt{D}} & \frac{1}{\sqrt{D}} \\
\frac{1}{\sqrt{2}} & \frac{-1}{\sqrt{2}} & 0 & \cdots & 0 & 0 \\
\frac{1}{\sqrt{6}} & \frac{1}{\sqrt{6}} & \frac{-2}{\sqrt{6}} & \cdots & 0 & 0 \\
\vdots & \vdots & \vdots & \cdots & \vdots & \vdots \\
\frac{1}{\sqrt{(D-2)+(D-2)^2}} & \frac{1}{\sqrt{(D-2)+(D-2)^2}} & \frac{1}{\sqrt{(D-2)+(D-2)^2}} & \cdots & \frac{-(D-2)}{\sqrt{(D-2)+(D-2)^2}} & 0 \\
\frac{1}{\sqrt{(D-1)+(D-1)^2}} & \frac{1}{\sqrt{(D-1)+(D-1)^2}} & \frac{1}{\sqrt{(D-1)+(D-1)^2}} & \cdots & \frac{1}{\sqrt{(D-1)+(D-1)^2}} & \frac{-(D-1)}{\sqrt{(D-1)+(D-1)^2}}
\end{pmatrix} \quad (12)
$$

5.4 Experimental results

Tables 3 and 4 show the experimental results on OBX and OBX2 for original functions and rotated functions, respectively. The mean value and the standard deviation of best objective values in 50 runs are shown for each function. The maximum number of evaluations is selected for each function and is shown in column labeled $FE_{\max}$. The best result among algorithms is highlighted using bold face fonts. Also, Wilcoxon signed rank test is performed and the result for each function is shown in parentheses. Symbols '+', '−' and '=' are shown when OBX/OBX2 is significantly better than BLX, is significantly worse than BLX, and is not significantly different from BLX, respectively. Symbols '++' and '−−' are shown when the significance level is 1% and '+' and '−' are shown when the significance level is 5%.

In original problems, OBX-0.5, OBX-0.6 and OBX-0.7 attained significantly better results than BLX-0.5 in 2 functions (f_3 and f_6), 4 functions (f_3, f_4, f_6 and f_7), and 3 functions (f_3, f_4 and f_5), respectively. BLX-0.5 attained significantly better results than OBX-0.5, OBX-0.6 and OBX-0.7 in 10 functions, 9 functions, and 9 functions, respectively. Also, OBX2-0.5, OBX2-0.6 and OBX2-0.7 attained significantly better results than BLX-0.5 in 3 functions (f_3, f_6 and f_7), 4 functions (f_3, f_4, f_6 and f_7), and 4 functions (f_3, f_4, f_5 and f_7), respectively. BLX-0.5 attained significantly better results than OBX2-0.5, OBX2-0.6 and OBX2-0.7 in 10 functions, 9 functions, and 9 functions, respectively. It is thought that BLX-0.5 is the best crossover and is followed by OBX2-0.6, OBX-0.6 and OBX2-0.7.

In rotated problems, OBX-0.5, OBX-0.6 and OBX-0.7 attained significantly better results than BLX-0.5 in 3 functions (f_3, f_6 and f_8), 6 functions (f_3, f_6, f_7, f_8, f_{12} and f_{13}), and 7 functions (f_2, f_3, f_5, f_7, f_8, f_{12} and f_{13}), respectively. BLX-0.5 attained significantly better results than OBX-0.5, OBX-0.6 and OBX-0.7 in 8 functions, 6 functions, and 5 functions, respectively. Also, OBX2-0.5, OBX2-0.6 and OBX2-0.7 attained significantly better results than BLX-0.5 in 6 functions (f_3, f_6, f_7, f_8, f_{12} and f_{13}), 7 functions (f_3, f_4, f_6, f_7, f_8, f_{12} and f_{13}), and 8 functions (f_2, f_3, f_4, f_5, f_7, f_8, f_{12} and f_{13}), respectively. BLX-0.5 attained significantly better results than OBX2-0.5, OBX2-0.6 and OBX2-0.7 in 7 functions, 4 functions, and 5 functions, respectively. It is thought that OBX2-0.6 and OBX2-0.7 are the best crossover and is followed by OBX-0.7, OBX-0.6 and BLX-0.5.

5.5 Combination of BLX and OBX/OBX2

From the experimental results, OBX2-0.6, OBX2-0.7 and OBX-0.7 are suitable to solve rotated problems or non-separable problems. BLX-0.5 is suitable to solve non-rotated problems or separable problems. Also, OBX-0.6, OBX2-0.6 and OBX2-0.7 are relatively better than other OBX/OBX2 in non-rotated problems.

Table 3. Results of OBX and OBX2 with changing α compared with BLX

	$FE_{\max}$	BLX-0.5	OBX-0.5	OBX-0.6	OBX-0.7
f_1	150,000	**8.24e-42 ± 4.80e-42**	6.12e-21 ± 1.20e-20 (--)	5.08e-29 ± 1.53e-28 (--)	7.11e-28 ± 1.74e-27 (--)
f_2	200,000	**5.80e-35 ± 2.42e-35**	4.62e-01 ± 3.38e-01 (--)	6.12e-02 ± 1.10e-01 (--)	4.75e-07 ± 3.11e-06 (--)
f_3	500,000	1.56e-02 ± 1.04e-02	9.80e-15 ± 1.67e-14 (++)	2.45e-35 ± 7.47e-35 (++)	**1.90e-46 ± 1.20e-45** (++)
f_4	500,000	7.21e-20 ± 9.80e-20	1.07e-01 ± 1.60e-01 (--)	6.76e-19 ± 2.76e-18 (++)	**3.62e-20 ± 2.19e-19** (++)
f_5	300,000	2.96e+01 ± 1.68e+01	3.66e+01 ± 3.16e+01 (--)	3.38e+01 ± 3.11e+01 (--)	**2.60e+01 ± 1.28e+01** (+)
f_6	10,000	5.92e+01 ± 1.02e+01	**2.53e+01 ± 1.25e+01** (++)	3.88e+01 ± 2.04e+01 (++)	1.16e+02 ± 3.68e+01 (--)
f_7	300,000	1.74e-03 ± 4.54e-04	1.86e-03 ± 8.35e-04 (=)	**1.54e-03 ± 6.00e-04** (+)	1.71e-03 ± 5.81e-04 (=)
f_8	100,000	**5.54e+03 ± 1.03e+03**	7.61e+03 ± 5.14e+02 (--)	7.66e+03 ± 4.10e+02 (--)	7.66e+03 ± 3.28e+02 (--)
f_9	100,000	**6.48e+01 ± 2.81e+01**	1.37e+02 ± 2.20e+01 (--)	1.58e+02 ± 1.44e+01 (--)	1.70e+02 ± 1.20e+01 (--)
f_{10}	50,000	**1.36e-06 ± 2.90e-07**	9.08e-01 ± 7.37e-01 (--)	1.65e-01 ± 4.11e-01 (--)	1.89e-02 ± 1.30e-01 (--)
f_{11}	50,000	**1.48e-04 ± 1.04e-03**	1.27e-02 ± 1.15e-02 (--)	4.48e-03 ± 6.80e-03 (--)	1.40e-03 ± 3.75e-03 (--)
f_{12}	50,000	**2.50e-11 ± 2.23e-11**	2.74e-02 ± 7.16e-02 (--)	1.59e-06 ± 1.09e-05 (--)	4.15e-03 ± 2.03e-02 (--)
f_{13}	50,000	**3.83e-10 ± 2.81e-10**	4.60e-03 ± 8.19e-03 (--)	1.54e-03 ± 3.81e-03 (--)	1.09e-04 ± 6.94e-04 (--)
+		—	2	4	3
=		—	1	0	1
−		—	10	9	9
	$FE_{\max}$	BLX-0.5	OBX2-0.5	OBX2-0.6	OBX2-0.7
f_1	150,000	**8.24e-42 ± 4.80e-42**	2.89e-22 ± 1.26e-21 (--)	3.82e-33 ± 1.18e-32 (--)	3.52e-32 ± 5.75e-32 (--)
f_2	200,000	**5.80e-35 ± 2.42e-35**	9.92e-02 ± 1.24e-01 (--)	1.46e-03 ± 4.03e-03 (--)	3.44e-19 ± 3.92e-19 (--)
f_3	500,000	1.56e-02 ± 1.04e-02	4.09e-14 ± 8.91e-14 (++)	2.38e-36 ± 5.08e-36 (++)	**4.87e-53 ± 1.67e-52** (++)
f_4	500,000	7.21e-20 ± 9.80e-20	2.29e-02 ± 3.50e-02 (--)	**2.17e-31 ± 2.90e-31** (++)	9.18e-28 ± 1.38e-27 (++)
f_5	300,000	2.96e+01 ± 1.68e+01	3.58e+01 ± 2.30e+01 (--)	3.52e+01 ± 4.68e+01 (--)	**2.37e+01 ± 1.09e+00** (+)
f_6	10,000	5.92e+01 ± 1.02e+01	**1.37e+01 ± 4.46e+00** (++)	2.73e+01 ± 7.63e+00 (++)	9.39e+01 ± 2.15e+01 (--)
f_7	300,000	1.74e-03 ± 4.54e-04	**1.18e-03 ± 4.40e-04** (++)	1.22e-03 ± 4.57e-04 (++)	1.34e-03 ± 4.03e-04 (++)
f_8	100,000	**5.54e+03 ± 1.03e+03**	7.80e+03 ± 3.75e+02 (--)	7.76e+03 ± 3.51e+02 (--)	7.59e+03 ± 4.01e+02 (--)
f_9	100,000	**6.48e+01 ± 2.81e+01**	1.60e+02 ± 1.02e+01 (--)	1.67e+02 ± 8.19e+00 (--)	1.73e+02 ± 8.34e+00 (--)
f_{10}	50,000	**1.36e-06 ± 2.90e-07**	8.02e-02 ± 2.69e-01 (--)	2.46e-05 ± 5.67e-05 (--)	4.94e-05 ± 1.97e-05 (--)
f_{11}	50,000	1.48e-04 ± 1.04e-03	4.60e-03 ± 6.42e-03 (--)	1.99e-03 ± 4.24e-03 (--)	**8.17e-06 ± 6.18e-06** (--)
f_{12}	50,000	**2.50e-11 ± 2.23e-11**	1.75e-06 ± 5.07e-06 (--)	1.96e-08 ± 1.08e-07 (--)	1.48e-08 ± 2.55e-08 (--)
f_{13}	50,000	**3.83e-10 ± 2.81e-10**	1.98e-03 ± 4.22e-03 (--)	4.40e-04 ± 2.15e-03 (--)	1.73e-07 ± 2.56e-07 (--)
+		—	3	4	4
=		—	0	0	0
−		—	10	9	9

Therefore, combination of OBX/OBX2 and BLX-0.5 might help to increase diversity of children and improve the performance of GA. In this study, stochastic combination of OBX/OBX2 and BLX-0.5 is proposed: OBX/OBX2 is selected with probability p and BLX-0.5 is selected with probability $1 - p$.

The experimental conditions are as follows: p is selected from 0.25, 0.5 and 0.75. OBX-0.6 and OBX2-0.6 are adopted. Other conditions are same as the previous experiments.

Tables 5 and 6 show the experimental results on OBX-0.6 with BLX-0.5 and OBX2-0.6 with BLX-0.5 for original functions and rotated functions, respectively.

In original problems, OBX-0.6 with p=0.25, 0.5, and 0.75 attained significantly better results than BLX-0.5 in 6 functions. BLX-0.5 attained significantly better results than OBX-0.6 with p=0.25, 0.5, and 0.75 in 7 functions. Also, OBX2-0.6 with p=0.25, 0.5, and 0.75 attained significantly better results than BLX-0.5 in 8 functions. BLX-0.5 attained significantly better results than OBX-0.6 with p=0.25, 0.5, and 0.75 in 5 functions. It is thought that OBX2-0.6 with p=0.25, 0.5, and 0.75 are the best crossover and is followed by BLX-0.5.

In rotated problems, OBX-0.6 with p=0.25, 0.5 and 0.75 attained significantly better results than BLX-0.5 in 11 functions out of 13 functions. BLX-0.5 attained significantly better results than OBX-0.6 with p=0.25, 0.5, and 0.75 in 0 function, 1 function (f_9), and 1 function, respectively. Also, OBX2-0.6 with p=0.25, 0.5, and 0.75 attained significantly better results than BLX-0.5 in 11 functions. BLX-0.5 attained significantly better results than OBX-0.6 with p=0.25, 0.5 and 0.75 in 1 function (f_9). It is thought that OBX2-0.6 with p=0.25 is the best crossover and is followed

Table 4. Results of OBX and OBX2 with changing α for rotated problems

	FE_{max}	BLX-0.5	OBX-0.5	OBX-0.6	OBX-0.7
f_1	150,000	**8.24e-42 ± 4.80e-42**	6.12e-21 ± 1.20e-20 (--)	5.08e-29 ± 1.53e-28 (--)	7.11e-28 ± 1.74e-27 (--)
f_2	200,000	1.28e-02 ± 6.48e-02	4.61e-01 ± 4.35e-01 (--)	5.38e-02 ± 9.91e-02 (--)	**2.74e-10 ± 1.63e-09** (++)
f_3	500,000	2.39e-02 ± 4.17e-02	1.03e-14 ± 2.28e-14 (++)	1.92e-34 ± 1.29e-33 (++)	**5.05e-47 ± 1.74e-46** (++)
f_4	500,000	**1.57e-21 ± 5.94e-21**	1.59e-01 ± 2.83e-01 (--)	1.85e-19 ± 6.21e-19 (--)	1.85e-21 ± 7.52e-21 (=)
f_5	300,000	3.32e+01 ± 2.06e+01	3.78e+01 ± 2.79e+01 (--)	3.55e+01 ± 2.71e+01 (=)	**2.81e+01 ± 1.60e+01** (++)
f_6	10,000	6.01e+01 ± 1.37e+01	**2.61e+01 ± 1.51e+01** (++)	3.68e+01 ± 1.39e+01 (++)	1.24e+02 ± 4.26e+01 (--)
f_7	300,000	1.75e-03 ± 3.55e-04	1.71e-03 ± 7.24e-04 (=)	1.52e-03 ± 6.42e-04 (++)	**1.58e-03 ± 5.18e-04** (+)
f_8	100,000	7.56e+03 ± 3.21e+02	6.94e+03 ± 4.76e+02 (++)	6.44e+03 ± 5.67e+02 (++)	**6.09e+03 ± 6.63e+02** (++)
f_9	100,000	**1.31e+02 ± 1.73e+01**	1.33e+02 ± 2.94e+01 (=)	1.57e+02 ± 1.09e+01 (--)	1.67e+02 ± 1.20e+01 (--)
f_{10}	50,000	**1.54e-06 ± 3.12e-07**	7.64e-01 ± 7.23e-01 (--)	2.39e-02 ± 1.62e-01 (--)	3.00e-04 ± 3.17e-04 (--)
f_{11}	50,000	**1.32e-05 ± 8.45e-05**	1.20e-02 ± 8.49e-03 (--)	4.71e-03 ± 6.96e-03 (--)	6.09e-04 ± 2.27e-03 (--)
f_{12}	50,000	8.36e-06 ± 2.76e-06	1.91e-02 ± 4.51e-02 (--)	2.07e-03 ± 1.45e-02 (++)	**2.38e-07 ± 5.76e-07** (++)
f_{13}	50,000	**1.16e-05 ± 3.21e-06**	3.52e-03 ± 5.54e-03 (−)	1.32e-03 ± 3.57e-03 (++)	4.41e-04 ± 2.15e-03 (++)
+		—	3	6	7
=		—	2	1	1
−		—	8	6	5

	FE_{max}	BLX-0.5	OBX2-0.5	OBX2-0.6	OBX2-0.7
f_1	150,000	**8.24e-42 ± 4.80e-42**	2.89e-22 ± 1.26e-21(--)	3.82e-33 ± 1.18e-32(--)	3.52e-32 ± 5.75e-32(--)
f_2	200,000	1.28e-02 ± 6.48e-02	1.20e-01 ± 1.64e-01(--)	7.15e-04 ± 3.51e-03(=)	**2.90e-19 ± 4.58e-19**(++)
f_3	500,000	2.39e-02 ± 4.17e-02	6.97e-14 ± 1.01e-13(++)	9.95e-36 ± 4.70e-35(++)	**1.37e-52 ± 3.38e-52**(++)
f_4	500,000	1.57e-21 ± 5.94e-21	1.83e-02 ± 2.41e-02(--)	**2.44e-31 ± 4.14e-31**(++)	1.02e-27 ± 1.66e-27(++)
f_5	300,000	3.32e+01 ± 2.06e+01	3.19e+01 ± 1.80e+01(-)	2.96e+01 ± 1.44e+01(=)	**2.52e+01 ± 7.79e+00**(++)
f_6	10,000	6.01e+01 ± 1.37e+01	**1.38e+01 ± 6.74e+00**(++)	2.88e+01 ± 9.08e+00(++)	9.62e+01 ± 2.50e+01(--)
f_7	300,000	1.75e-03 ± 3.55e-04	**1.18e-03 ± 4.49e-04**(++)	1.27e-03 ± 4.06e-04(++)	1.48e-03 ± 4.92e-04(++)
f_8	100,000	7.56e+03 ± 3.21e+02	6.06e+03 ± 1.29e+03(++)	5.63e+03 ± 6.61e+02(++)	**5.39e+03 ± 7.89e+02**(++)
f_9	100,000	**1.31e+02 ± 1.73e+01**	1.61e+02 ± 9.14e+00(--)	1.62e+02 ± 1.09e+01(--)	1.74e+02 ± 9.61e+00(--)
f_{10}	50,000	**1.54e-06 ± 3.12e-07**	4.07e-03 ± 2.07e-02(--)	2.28e-05 ± 3.11e-05(--)	4.66e-05 ± 2.02e-05(--)
f_{11}	50,000	**1.32e-05 ± 8.45e-05**	6.57e-03 ± 7.61e-03(--)	2.74e-03 ± 5.72e-03(--)	4.33e-05 ± 2.30e-04(--)
f_{12}	50,000	8.36e-06 ± 2.76e-06	8.02e-07 ± 1.97e-06(++)	**2.28e-09 ± 4.01e-09**(++)	1.90e-08 ± 2.95e-08(++)
f_{13}	50,000	1.16e-05 ± 3.21e-06	1.32e-03 ± 3.57e-03(+)	**1.19e-06 ± 5.82e-06**(++)	4.10e-06 ± 2.77e-05(++)
+		—	6	7	8
=		—	0	2	0
−		—	7	4	5

by other OBX/OBX2 with p but the difference is very small.

As a whole, it is thought that OBX2 with p=0.25, 0.5 and 0.75 is the best method.

As a reference, Figures 6 to 10 and Figures 11 to 15 show the change of best objective value found for BLX-0.5 and OBX2-0.6 with p=0.25, 0.5 and 0.75 within 100,000 function evaluations.

6. Conclusion

In this study, we proposed new rotation-invariant and two-parent crossover operations called OBX and OBX2, where an oblique coordinate system is built using a population and a blend crossover along the oblique coordinate system is performed.

GA with OBX/OBX2 is applied to optimization of various 13 functions including unimodal functions, a function with ridge structure, multimodal functions. Also, it is applied to solve their rotated problems. It is shown that OBX/OBX2 is not effective to the original problems but is effective to rotated problems compared with BLX. Therefore, we proposed to combine OBX/OBX2 with BLX stochastically. It is shown that OBX2 with BLX is effective to both of the original problems and the rotated problems compared with BLX.

Future work includes the followings:

1. In this study, the probability parameter p is fixed. A proper parameter value will be changed according to problems to be solved and according to the state of search. We will introduce dynamic control of p to improve the performance of our method. It is thought that success-

Table 5. Results of OBX-0.6 and OBX2-0.6 with changing p compared with BLX

	FE_{max}	BLX-0.5	OBX-0.6 (p=0.25)	OBX-0.6 (p=0.5)	OBX-0.6 (p=0.75)
f_1	150,000	8.24e-42 ± 4.80e-42	8.07e-44 ± 6.98e-44 (++)	**5.37e-45 ± 7.29e-45 (++)**	2.24e-42 ± 3.81e-42 (++)
f_2	200,000	**5.80e-35 ± 2.42e-35**	9.47e-04 ± 4.02e-03 (--)	1.25e-03 ± 7.16e-03 (--)	2.98e-04 ± 1.37e-03 (--)
f_3	500,000	1.56e-02 ± 1.04e-02	4.87e-13 ± 9.29e-13 (++)	5.72e-23 ± 2.64e-22 (++)	**2.25e-31 ± 9.63e-31 (++)**
f_4	500,000	7.21e-20 ± 9.80e-20	5.36e-26 ± 2.34e-25 (++)	1.64e-24 ± 6.11e-24 (++)	**8.81e-27 ± 2.80e-26 (++)**
f_5	300,000	2.96e+01 ± 1.68e+01	2.87e+01 ± 1.39e+01 (−)	**2.67e+01 ± 7.93e+00 (--)**	2.81e+01 ± 1.15e+01 (--)
f_6	10,000	5.92e+01 ± 1.02e+01	3.96e+01 ± 8.43e+00 (++)	2.42e+01 ± 4.85e+00 (++)	**2.09e+01 ± 8.39e+00 (++)**
f_7	300,000	1.74e-03 ± 4.54e-04	1.37e-03 ± 3.51e-04 (++)	1.22e-03 ± 3.51e-04 (++)	**1.08e-03 ± 3.21e-04 (++)**
f_8	100,000	**5.54e+03 ± 1.03e+03**	7.39e+03 ± 3.58e+02 (--)	7.12e+03 ± 4.00e+02 (--)	6.79e+03 ± 4.05e+02 (--)
f_9	100,000	**6.48e+01 ± 2.81e+01**	1.33e+02 ± 1.93e+01 (--)	1.47e+02 ± 1.58e+01 (--)	1.52e+02 ± 1.09e+01 (--)
f_{10}	50,000	1.36e-06 ± 2.90e-07	7.54e-07 ± 1.65e-07 (++)	**4.42e-07 ± 1.25e-07 (++)**	7.99e-07 ± 3.54e-07 (++)
f_{11}	50,000	1.48e-04 ± 1.04e-03	1.18e-07 ± 2.88e-07 (--)	**3.53e-08 ± 3.82e-08 (--)**	7.88e-04 ± 3.21e-03 (--)
f_{12}	50,000	**2.50e-11 ± 2.23e-11**	8.81e-08 ± 4.24e-08 (--)	2.85e-09 ± 1.74e-09 (--)	1.16e-09 ± 2.44e-09 (--)
f_{13}	50,000	**3.83e-10 ± 2.81e-10**	2.13e-07 ± 8.80e-08 (--)	1.03e-08 ± 6.73e-09 (--)	2.20e-04 ± 1.54e-03 (--)
+		—	6	6	6
=		—	0	0	0
−		—	7	7	7
	FE_{max}	BLX-0.5	OBX2-0.6 (p=0.25)	OBX2-0.6 (p=0.5)	OBX2-0.6 (p=0.75)
f_1	150,000	8.24e-42 ± 4.80e-42	3.23e-43 ± 2.38e-43(++)	**2.91e-44 ± 2.31e-44(++)**	6.53e-43 ± 1.02e-42(++)
f_2	200,000	**5.80e-35 ± 2.42e-35**	3.83e-32 ± 1.69e-32(--)	2.44e-30 ± 9.23e-31(--)	1.02e-28 ± 6.58e-29(--)
f_3	500,000	1.56e-02 ± 1.04e-02	1.75e-12 ± 2.89e-12(++)	5.03e-22 ± 2.20e-21(++)	**3.64e-30 ± 2.02e-29(++)**
f_4	500,000	7.21e-20 ± 9.80e-20	1.84e-25 ± 3.31e-25(++)	1.61e-27 ± 5.64e-27(++)	**1.52e-29 ± 3.38e-29(++)**
f_5	300,000	2.96e+01 ± 1.68e+01	2.58e+01 ± 7.82e+00(--)	**2.52e+01 ± 9.50e-01(--)**	2.54e+01 ± 6.03e-01(--)
f_6	10,000	5.92e+01 ± 1.02e+01	4.09e+01 ± 8.34e+00(++)	3.09e+01 ± 6.72e+00(++)	**2.44e+01 ± 4.88e+00(++)**
f_7	300,000	1.74e-03 ± 4.54e-04	1.44e-03 ± 3.27e-04(++)	1.19e-03 ± 3.25e-04(++)	**1.10e-03 ± 3.09e-04(++)**
f_8	100,000	**5.54e+03 ± 1.03e+03**	6.11e+03 ± 1.10e+03(--)	6.70e+03 ± 5.47e+02(--)	7.22e+03 ± 3.54e+02(--)
f_9	100,000	**6.48e+01 ± 2.81e+01**	8.93e+01 ± 1.89e+01(--)	1.17e+02 ± 1.76e+01(--)	1.38e+02 ± 1.24e+01(--)
f_{10}	50,000	1.36e-06 ± 2.90e-07	8.66e-07 ± 1.60e-07(++)	**6.06e-07 ± 1.46e-07(++)**	7.58e-07 ± 2.59e-07(++)
f_{11}	50,000	1.48e-04 ± 1.04e-03	**1.85e-10 ± 8.50e-11(--)**	6.02e-07 ± 4.22e-06(--)	1.48e-04 ± 1.04e-03(--)
f_{12}	50,000	2.50e-11 ± 2.23e-11	3.51e-12 ± 2.01e-12(++)	**1.40e-12 ± 8.74e-13(++)**	3.04e-12 ± 3.13e-12(++)
f_{13}	50,000	3.83e-10 ± 2.81e-10	3.28e-11 ± 2.07e-11(++)	**1.69e-11 ± 1.19e-11(++)**	3.59e-11 ± 2.58e-11(++)
+		—	8	8	8
=		—	0	0	0
−		—	5	5	5

based tuning can be adopted: The success probability when the child is better than the parent is obtained for BLX and OBX separately. p is tuned as the crossover operation with higher success probability is often selected.

2. We will introduce the idea of OBX and OBX2 into other population-based optimization algorithms including differential evolution and particle swarm optimization.

Acknowledgment

This study is supported by JSPS KAKENHI Grant Numbers 26350443 and 17K00311.

References

[1] Goldberg, D. E., *Genetic Algorithms in Search, Optimization, and Machine Learning*, Addison Wesley (1989).

[2] Storn, R. and Price, K., "Minimizing the Real Functions of the ICEC'96 Contest by Differential Evolution", *Proc. of the International Conference on Evolutionary Computation* (1996), pp. 842–844.

[3] Storn, R. and Price, K., "Differential Evolution – A Simple and Efficient Heuristic for Global Optimization over Continuous Spaces", *Journal of Global Optimization*, Vol. 11, pp. 341–359 (1997).

Table 6. Results of OBX-0.6 and OBX2-0.6 with changing p for rotated problems

	FE_{max}	BLX-0.5	OBX-0.6 (p=0.25)	OBX-0.6 (p=0.5)	OBX-0.6 (p=0.75)
f_1	150,000	8.24e-42 ± 4.80e-42	8.07e-44 ± 6.98e-44 (++)	**5.37e-45 ± 7.29e-45 (++)**	2.24e-42 ± 3.81e-42 (++)
f_2	200,000	1.28e-02 ± 6.48e-02	9.47e-04 ± 4.02e-03 (++)	1.25e-03 ± 7.16e-03 (++)	**2.98e-04 ± 1.37e-03 (+)**
f_3	500,000	2.39e-02 ± 4.17e-02	4.87e-13 ± 9.29e-13 (++)	5.72e-23 ± 2.64e-22 (++)	**2.25e-31 ± 9.63e-31 (++)**
f_4	500,000	1.57e-21 ± 5.94e-21	5.36e-26 ± 2.34e-25 (++)	1.64e-24 ± 6.11e-24 (++)	**8.81e-27 ± 2.80e-26 (++)**
f_5	300,000	3.32e+01 ± 2.06e+01	2.87e+01 ± 1.39e+01 (=)	**2.67e+01 ± 7.93e+00 (=)**	2.81e+01 ± 1.15e+01 (=)
f_6	10,000	6.01e+01 ± 1.37e+01	3.96e+01 ± 8.43e+00 (++)	2.42e+01 ± 4.85e+00 (++)	**2.09e+01 ± 8.39e+00 (++)**
f_7	300,000	1.75e-03 ± 3.55e-04	1.37e-03 ± 3.51e-04 (++)	1.22e-03 ± 3.51e-04 (++)	**1.08e-03 ± 3.21e-04 (++)**
f_8	100,000	7.56e+03 ± 3.21e+02	7.39e+03 ± 3.58e+02 (+)	7.12e+03 ± 4.00e+02 (++)	**6.79e+03 ± 4.05e+02 (++)**
f_9	100,000	**1.31e+02 ± 1.73e+01**	1.33e+02 ± 1.93e+01 (=)	1.47e+02 ± 1.58e+01 (--)	1.52e+02 ± 1.09e+01 (--)
f_{10}	50,000	1.54e-06 ± 3.12e-07	7.54e-07 ± 1.65e-07 (++)	**4.42e-07 ± 1.25e-07 (++)**	7.99e-07 ± 3.54e-07 (++)
f_{11}	50,000	1.32e-05 ± 8.45e-05	1.18e-07 ± 2.88e-07 (++)	**3.53e-08 ± 3.82e-08 (++)**	7.88e-04 ± 3.21e-03 (++)
f_{12}	50,000	8.36e-06 ± 2.76e-06	8.81e-08 ± 4.24e-08 (++)	2.85e-09 ± 1.74e-09 (++)	**1.16e-09 ± 2.44e-09 (++)**
f_{13}	50,000	1.16e-05 ± 3.21e-06	2.13e-07 ± 8.80e-08 (++)	**1.03e-08 ± 6.73e-09 (++)**	2.20e-04 ± 1.54e-03 (++)
+		—	11	11	11
=		—	2	1	1
−		—	0	1	1
	FE_{max}	BLX-0.5	OBX2-0.6 (p=0.25)	OBX2-0.6 (p=0.5)	OBX2-0.6 (p=0.75)
f_1	150,000	8.24e-42 ± 4.80e-42	3.23e-43 ± 2.38e-43(++)	**2.91e-44 ± 2.31e-44(++)**	6.53e-43 ± 1.02e-42(++)
f_2	200,000	1.28e-02 ± 6.48e-02	1.49e-03 ± 1.04e-02(++)	9.38e-05 ± 6.41e-04(++)	**3.39e-06 ± 2.37e-05(++)**
f_3	500,000	2.39e-02 ± 4.17e-02	7.46e-14 ± 1.18e-13(++)	1.06e-23 ± 2.05e-23(++)	**1.03e-30 ± 2.66e-30(++)**
f_4	500,000	1.57e-21 ± 5.94e-21	4.75e-28 ± 9.09e-28(++)	9.36e-30 ± 5.30e-29(++)	**3.83e-31 ± 9.84e-31(++)**
f_5	300,000	3.32e+01 ± 2.06e+01	3.23e+01 ± 2.19e+01(=)	2.67e+01 ± 7.90e+00(=)	**2.59e+01 ± 1.03e+00(=)**
f_6	10,000	6.01e+01 ± 1.37e+01	4.12e+01 ± 6.80e+00(++)	3.04e+01 ± 7.79e+00(++)	**2.38e+01 ± 6.63e+00(++)**
f_7	300,000	1.75e-03 ± 3.55e-04	1.48e-03 ± 4.23e-04(++)	1.30e-03 ± 3.33e-04(++)	**1.10e-03 ± 3.13e-04(++)**
f_8	100,000	7.56e+03 ± 3.21e+02	7.38e+03 ± 3.28e+02(++)	7.22e+03 ± 3.79e+02(++)	**6.70e+03 ± 5.71e+02(++)**
f_9	100,000	**1.31e+02 ± 1.73e+01**	1.38e+02 ± 1.70e+01(-)	1.53e+02 ± 1.03e+01(--)	1.56e+02 ± 1.23e+01(--)
f_{10}	50,000	1.54e-06 ± 3.12e-07	8.90e-07 ± 2.07e-07(++)	**6.19e-07 ± 1.79e-07(++)**	7.92e-07 ± 2.70e-07(++)
f_{11}	50,000	1.32e-05 ± 8.45e-05	9.92e-08 ± 1.28e-07(++)	**3.26e-08 ± 5.88e-08(++)**	5.28e-06 ± 3.66e-05(++)
f_{12}	50,000	8.36e-06 ± 2.76e-06	1.80e-07 ± 7.95e-08(++)	6.50e-09 ± 4.62e-09(++)	**1.00e-09 ± 1.21e-09(++)**
f_{13}	50,000	1.16e-05 ± 3.21e-06	4.11e-07 ± 1.81e-07(++)	**2.29e-08 ± 1.54e-08(++)**	2.57e-07 ± 1.76e-06(++)
+		—	11	11	11
=		—	1	1	1
−		—	1	1	1

[4] Price, K., Storn, R. and Lampinen, J. A., *Differential Evolution: A Practical Approach to Global Optimization*, Springer (2005).

[5] Chakraborty, U. K. (ed.), *Advances in Differential Evolution*, Springer (2008).

[6] Das, S. and Suganthan, P., "Differential Evolution: A Survey of the State-of-the-Art", *IEEE Transactions on Evolutionary Computation*, Vol. 15, No. 1, pp. 4–31 (2011).

[7] Eshelman, L. J. and Schaffer, J. D., "Real-Coded Genetic Algorithms and Interval Schemata", Whitley, L. D. (ed.), *Foundations of Genetic Algorithms 2*, San Mateo, CA: Morgan Kaufmann Publishers, pp. 187–202 (1993).

[8] Deb, K. and Agrawal, R. B., "Simulated binary crossover for continuous search space", *Complex systems*, Vol. 9, No. 2, pp. 115–148 (1995).

[9] Takahama, T. and Sakai, S., "Solving Nonlinear Optimization Problems by Differential Evolution with a Rotation-Invariant Crossover Operation using Gram-Schmidt process", *Proc. of Second World Congress on Nature and Biologically Inspired Computing (NaBIC2010)* (2010), pp. 533–540.

[10] Guo, S.-M. and Yang, C.-C., "Enhancing differential evolution utilizing eigenvector-based crossover operator", *IEEE Transactions on Evolutionary Computation*, Vol. 19, No. 1, pp. 31–49 (2015).

[11] Higuchi, T., Tsutsui, S. and Yamamura, M., "Simplex Crossover of Real-Coded Genetic Algorithms", *Trans. of the Japanese Society of Artificial Intelligence*, Vol. 16, No. 3, pp. 147–155 (2001), in Japanese.

[12] Akimoto, Y., Nagata, Y., Sakuma, J., Ono, I. and Kobayashi, S., "Proposal and Evaluation of Adaptive Real-coded Crossover AREX", *Trans. of the Japanese Society of Artificial Intelligence*, Vol. 24, No. 6, pp. 446–458 (2009), in Japanese.

[13] Ono, I. and Kobayashi, S., "A Real Coded Genetic Algorithm for Function Optimization Using Unimodal Normal Distributed Crossover", *Proc. of the 7th International Conference on Genetic Algorithms* (1997), pp. 246–253.

[14] Tsutsui, S., Yamamura, M. and Higuchi, T., "Multi-Parent Recombination with Simplex Crossover in Real Coded Genetic Algorithms", *Proc. of Genetic and Evolutionary Computation Conference(GECCO'99)* (1999), pp. 657–664.

[15] Kobayashi, S., "The Frontiers of Real-Coded Genetic Algorithms", *Journal of Japanese Society for Artificial Intelligence*, Vol. 24, No. 1, pp. 147–162 (2009), in Japanese.

[16] Zhang, J. and Sanderson, A. C., "JADE: Adaptive Differential Evolution With Optional External Archive", *IEEE Transactions on Evolutionary Computation*, Vol. 13, No. 5, pp. 945–958 (2009).

[17] Shang, Y.-W. and Qiu, Y.-H., "A Note on the Extended Rosenbrock Function", *Evolutionary Computation*, Vol. 14, No. 1, pp. 119–126 (2006).

[18] Yao, X., Liu, Y., and Lin, G., "Evolutionary Programming Made Faster", *IEEE Transactions on Evolutionary Computation*, Vol. 3, pp. 82–102 (1999).

[19] Yao, X., Liu, Y., Liang, K.-H. and Lin, G., "Fast Evolutionary Algorithms", Ghosh, A. and Tsutsui, S. (eds.), *Advances in Evolutionary Computing: Theory and Applications*, New York, NY, USA: Springer-Verlag New York, Inc., pp. 45–94 (2003).

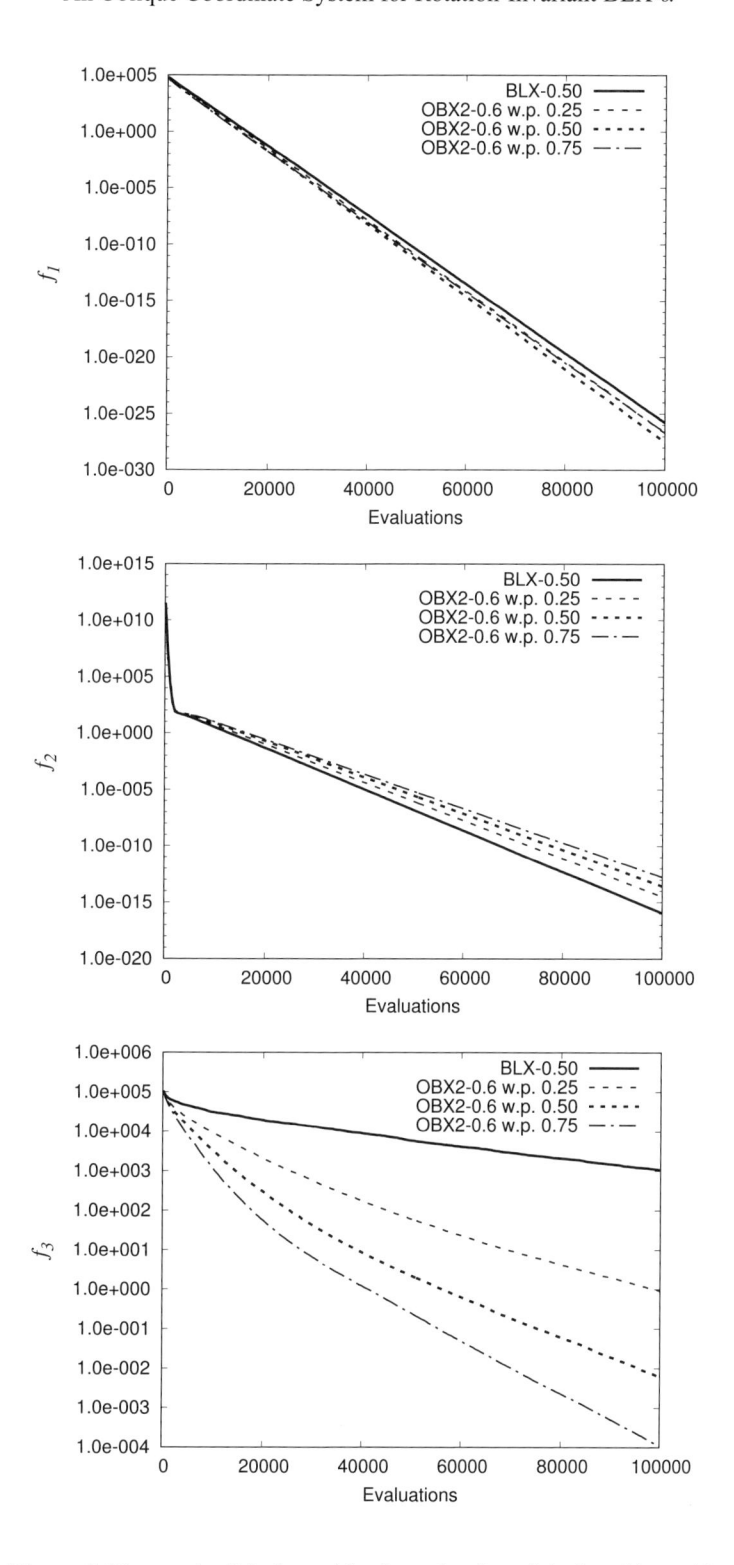

Figure 6. The graph of the best objective value for original problems (a)

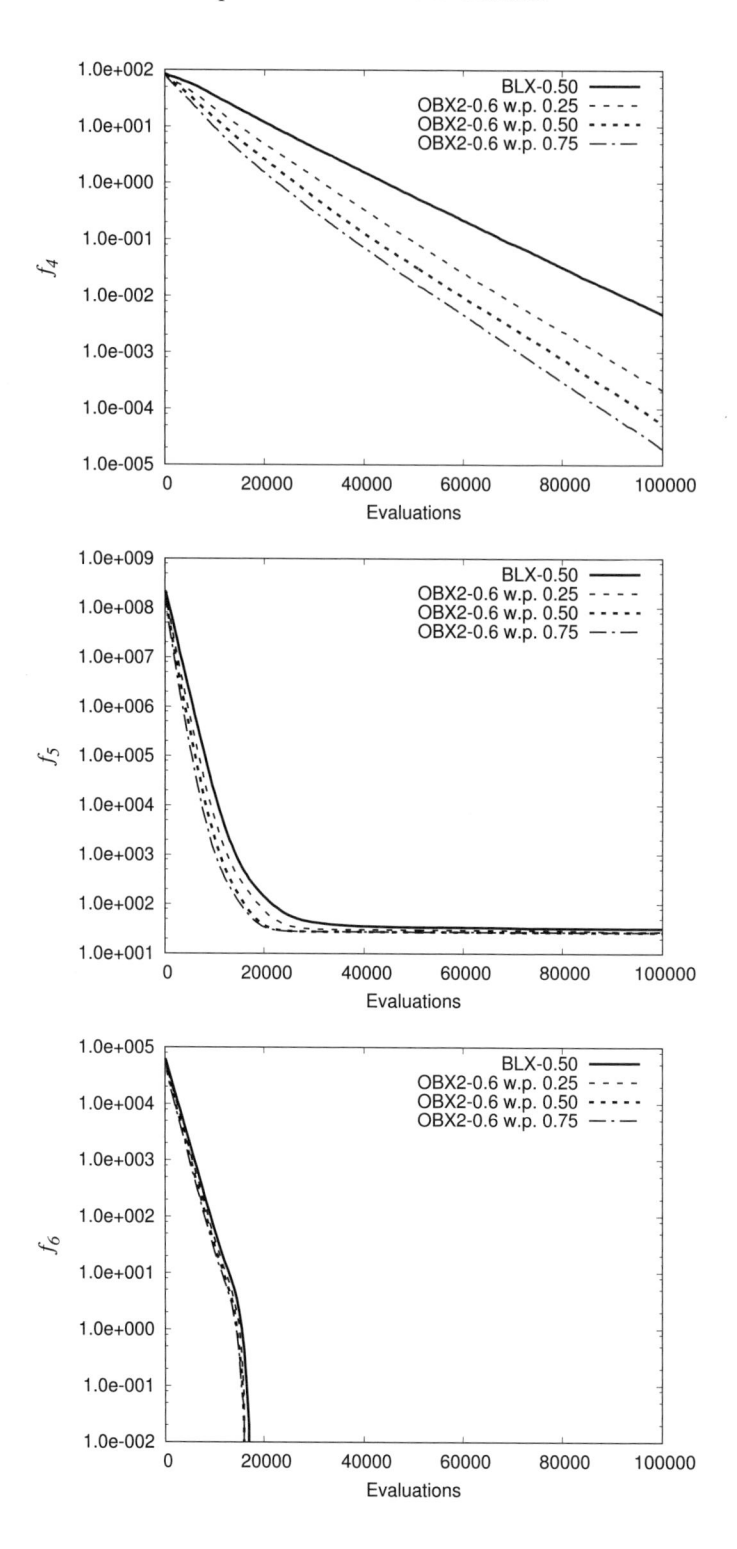

Figure 7. The graph of the best objective value for original problems (b)

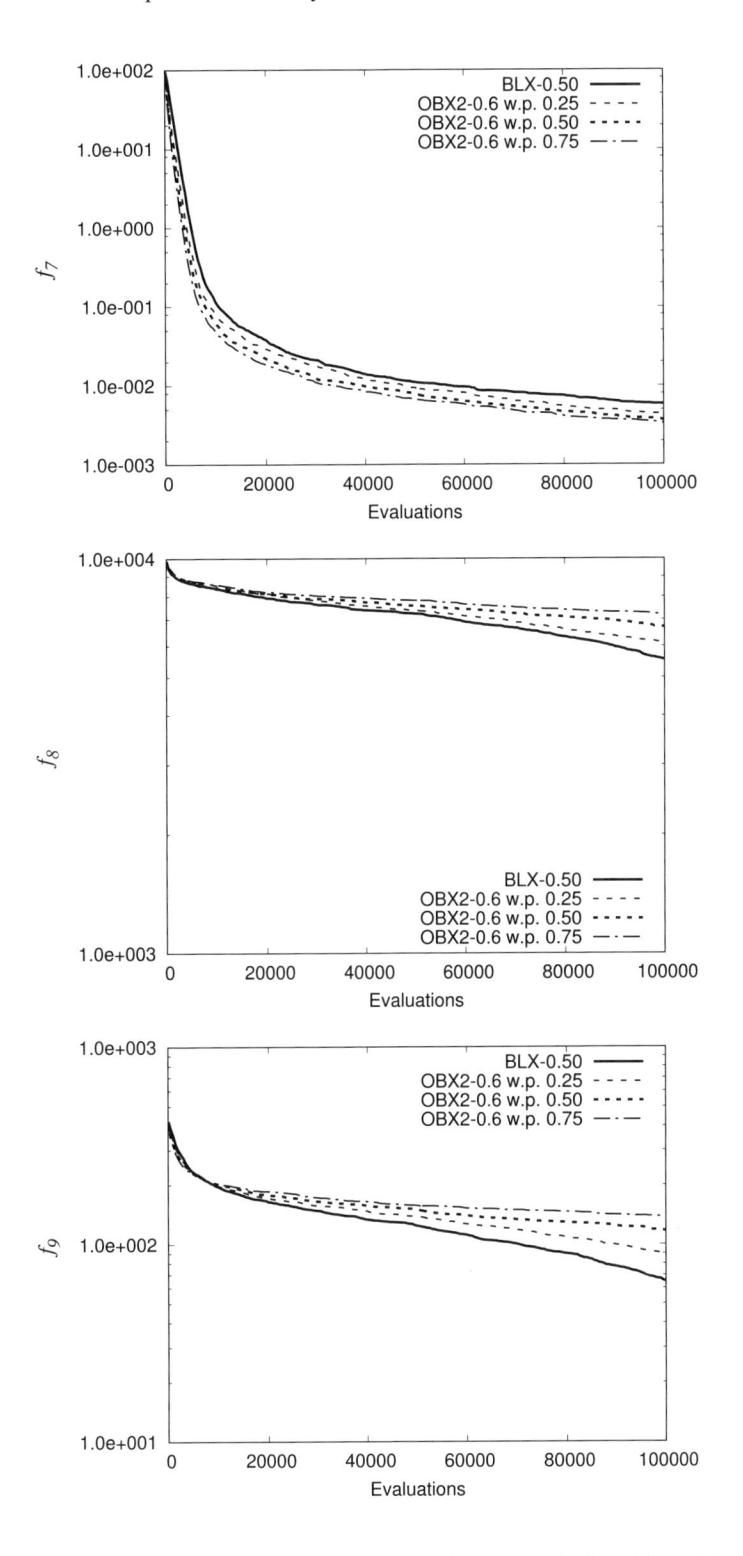

Figure 8. The graph of the best objective value for original problems (c)

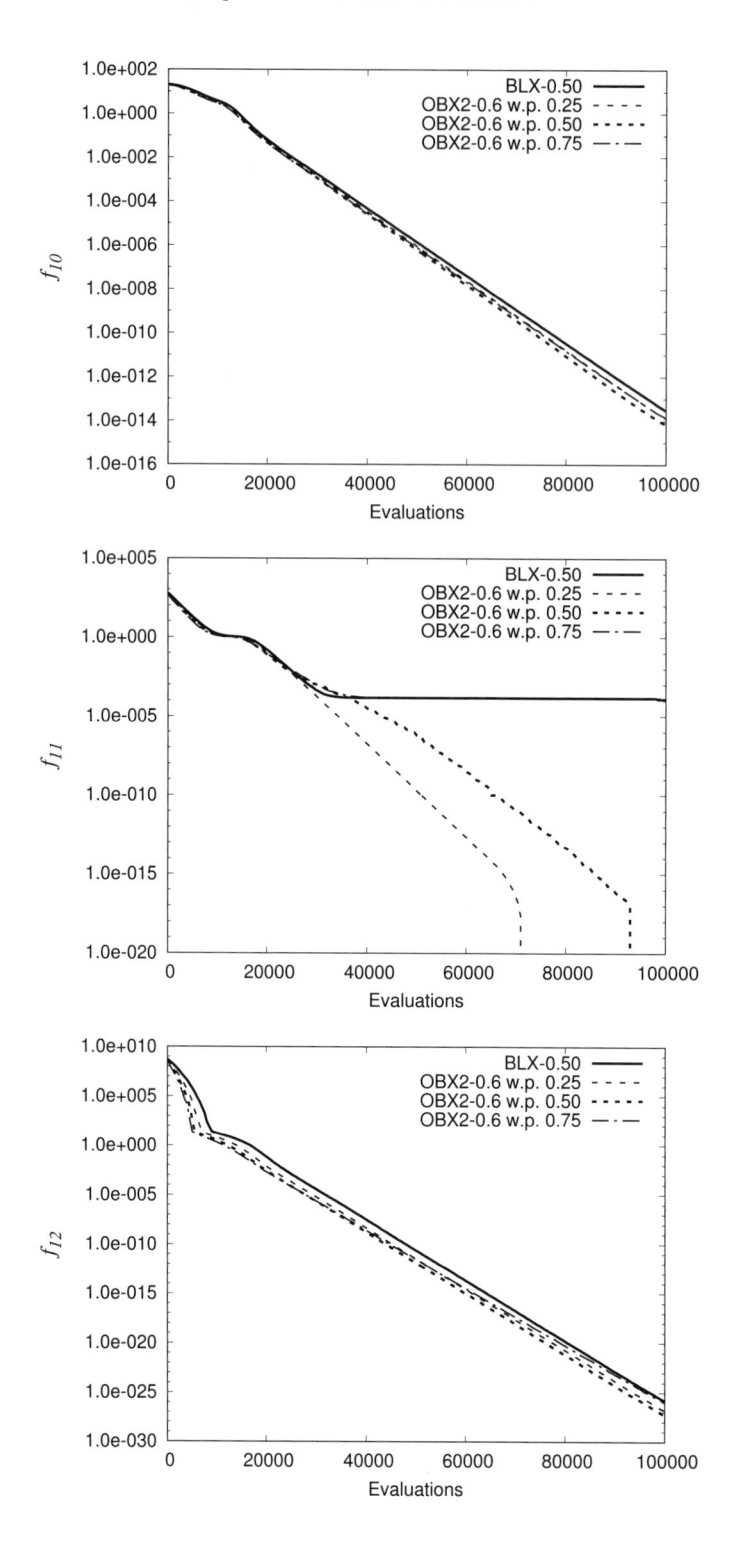

Figure 9. The graph of the best objective value for original problems (d)

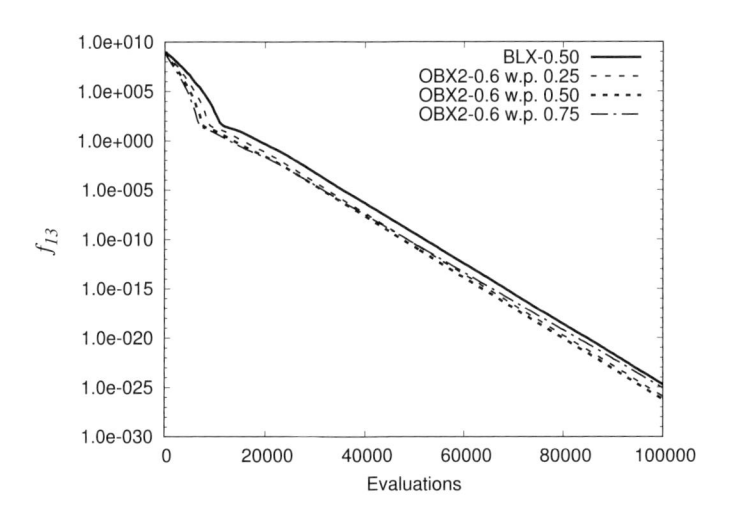

Figure 10. The graph of the best objective value for original problems (e)

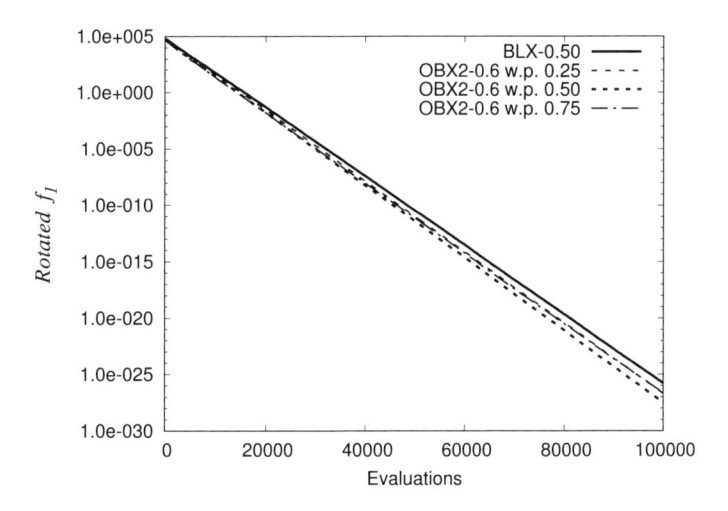

Figure 11. The graph of the best objective value for rotated problems (a)

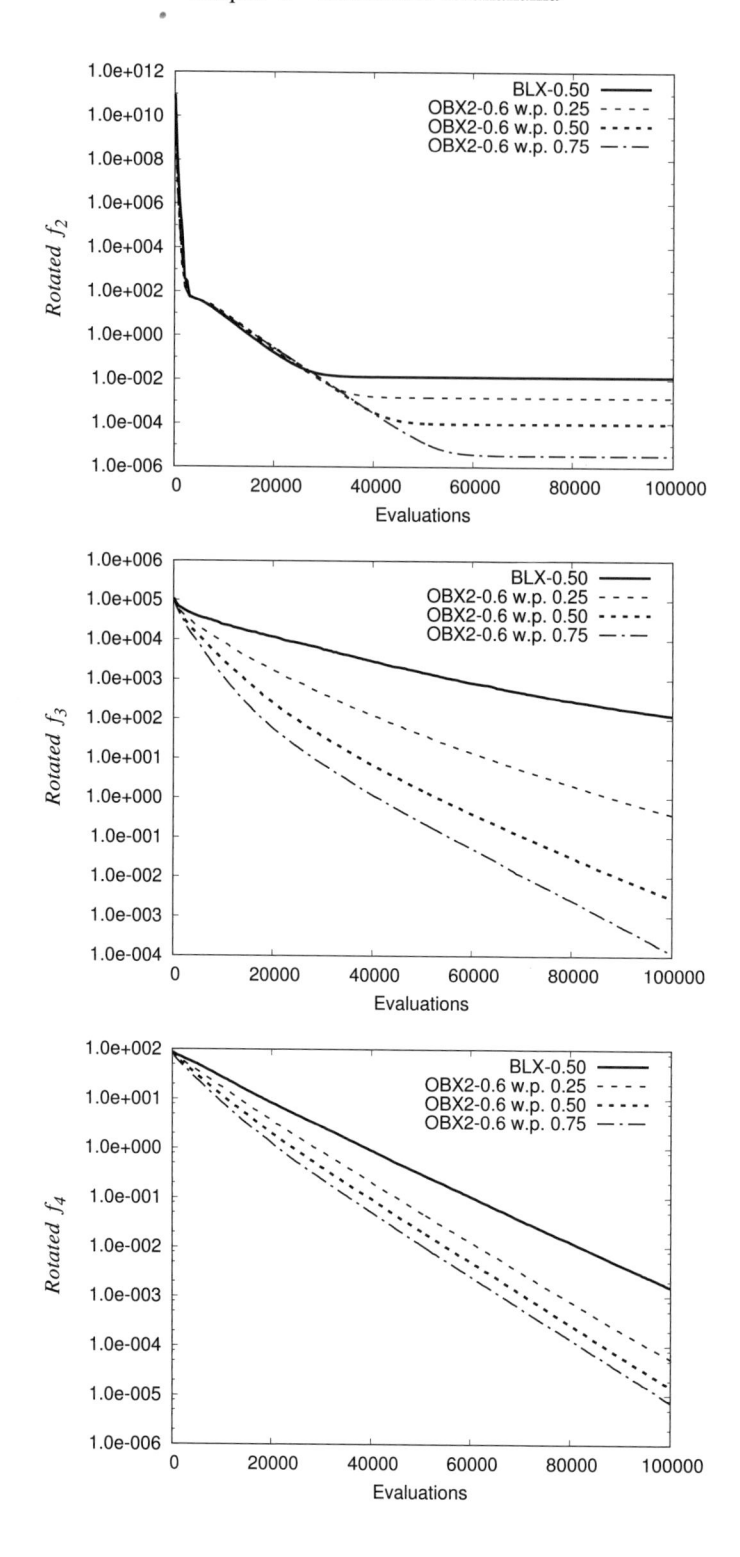

Figure 12. The graph of the best objective value for rotated problems (b)

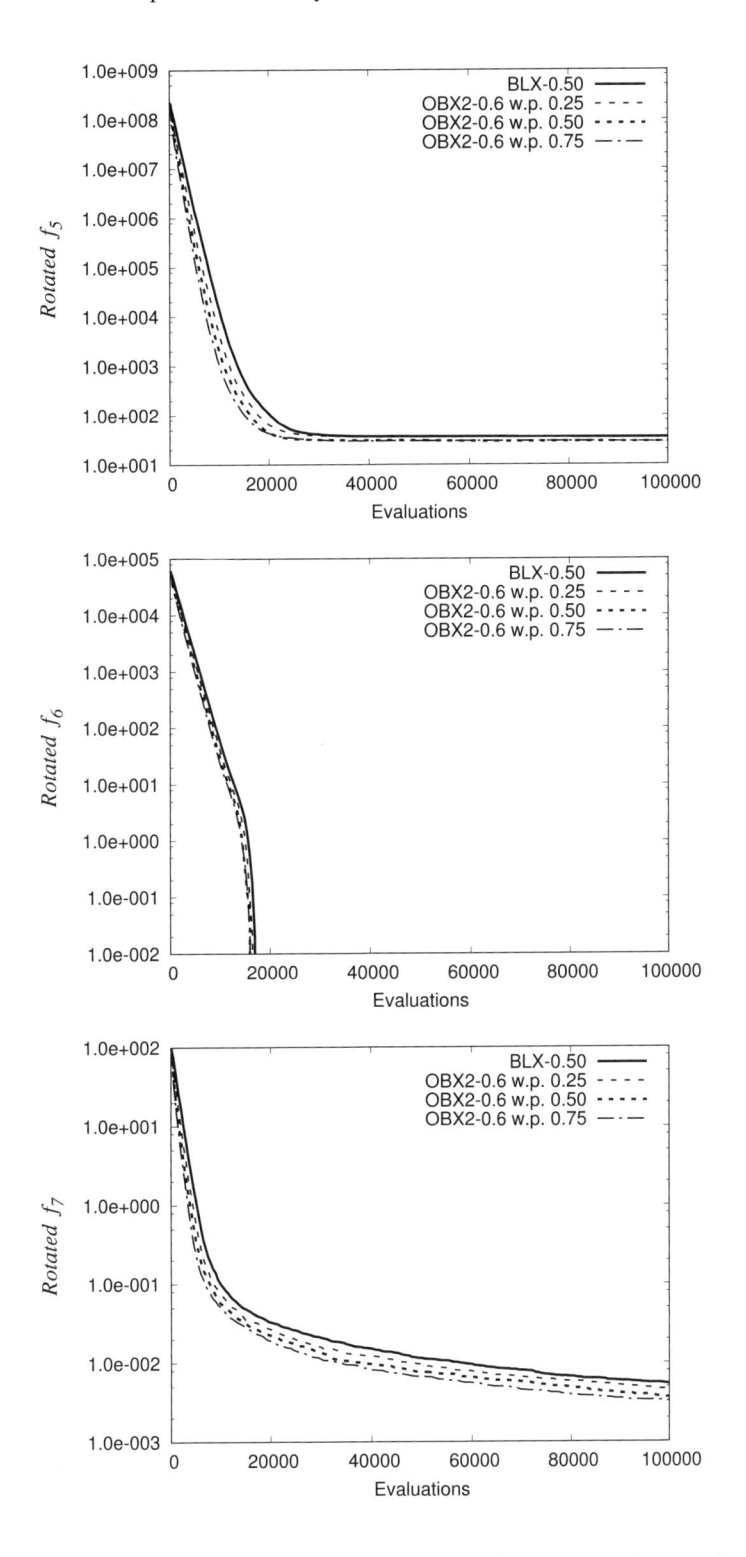

Figure 13. The graph of the best objective value for rotated problems (c)

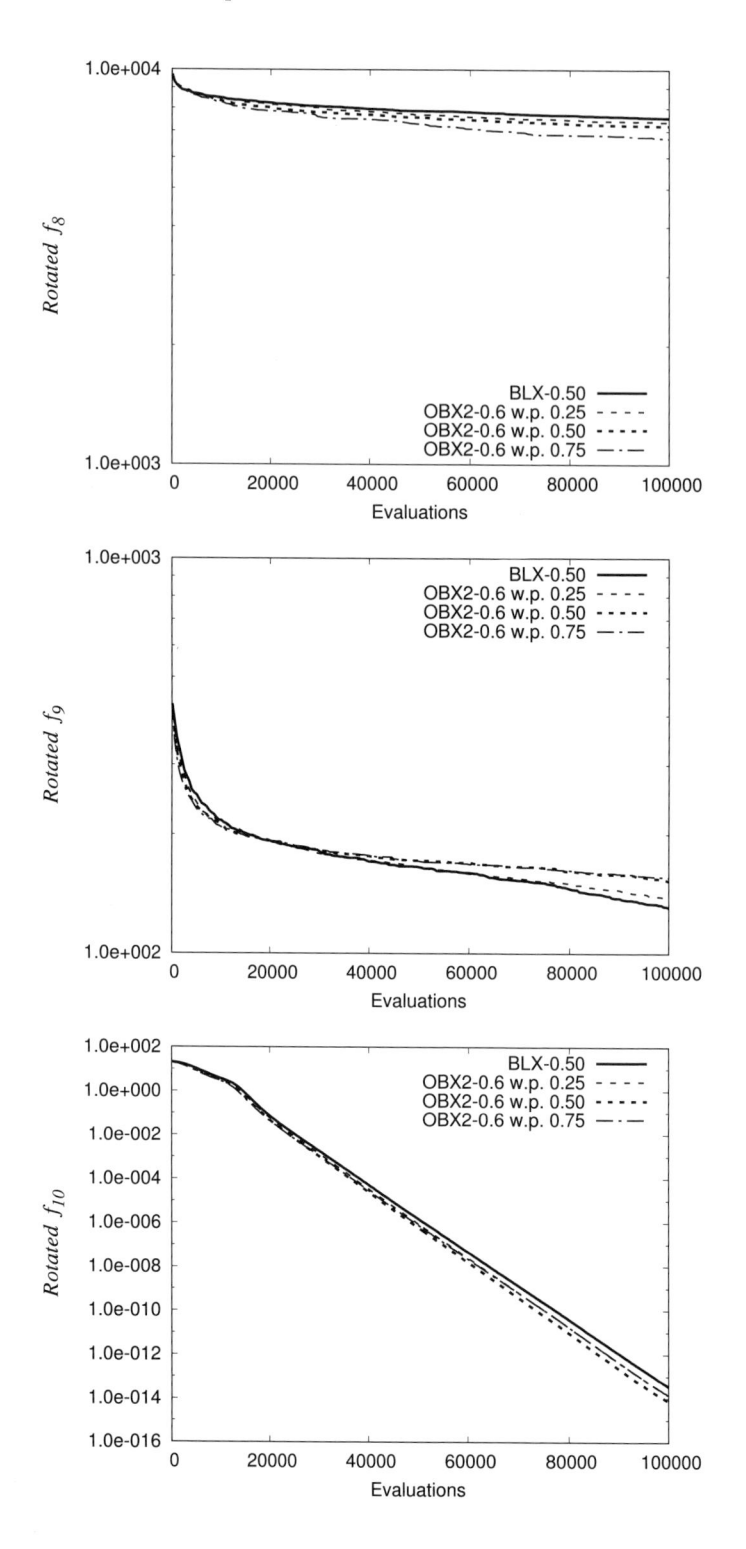

Figure 14. The graph of the best objective value for rotated problems (d)

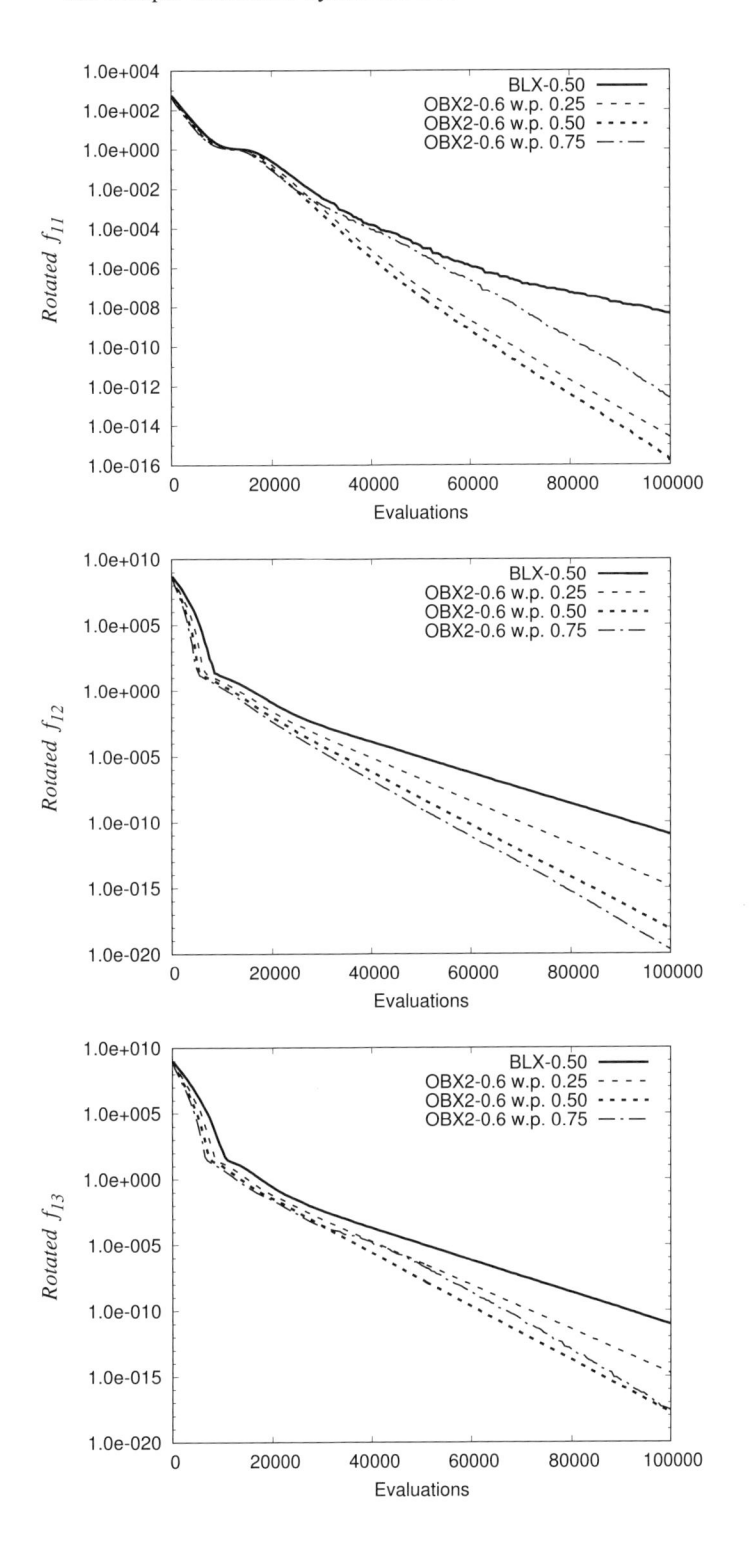

Figure 15. The graph of the best objective value for rotated problems (e)

Chapter 6

A Review of the Literature on Relationship Banking and SMEs

Yajing Liu[†]

Faculty of Economic Sciences, Hiroshima Shudo University,
1-1 Ozuka-Higashi 1-chome, Asaminami-ku, Hiroshima 731-3159, Japan

Abstract

This paper reviews the contemporary literature on relationship banking and small and medium enterprises (SMEs). We focus particularly on how reliable information is gathered though relationship banking to help SMEs succeed in obtaining funding, which can address the financial difficulties faced by SMEs. We also examine the development of relationship banking after the global financial crisis in 2008, and how relationship banking helped SMEs deal with the crisis, thus reducing the number of defaults. Finally, we look at how relationship banking has evolved since the financial crisis as a result of the distinct changes in two factors : Information technology and the economic environment, which have affected the value of soft information.

Keywords:

Relationship banking, SMEs, soft information, asymmetric information, financial crisis

1. Introduction

1.1 Definitions of Relationship Banking

Relationship banking is one of the main topics discussed in banking literatures. One of the most representative papers is by Petersen and Rajan (1994, 1995), but many researchers have examined how the relationships between banks and SME borrowers affects the funding conditions of SMEs, including interest rates and maturities. Generally speaking, they found that

---

[†] Yajing Liu is also a researcher of Graduate School of Economics, Kobe University.

relationship can help banking could alleviate the financial difficulties of SMEs (Elsas and Krahnen (1998), Angelini, Salvo, and Ferri (1998), Kim, Kristiansen, and Vale (2007), and Sakai, Uesugi, and Watanabe (2010)).

Relationship banking (also called "relationship lending" in some papers) has been defined in many ways. Smith and Ongena (1998) define the relationship banking as "the connection between a bank and customer that goes beyond the execution of simple, anonymous, financial transactions". Boot (2000) considered relationship banking to be the provision of a financial intermediary: "(1) investing in obtaining customer-specific information, often proprietary in nature; and (2) evaluating the profitability of these investments through multiple interactions with the same customer over time or products." Berger and Udell (2002) argue that "relationship lending is generally associated with the collection of soft information[1] over time through relationships between the bank and the firm or between the loan officer and the firm's owner." Soft information is difficult to completely summarize in a numeric score, such as the characters and reliability of a firm manager, or if a firm has a profitable future. Unlike soft information, hard information is based on objective criteria, such as financial disclosures, accounting reports, and default histories, etc.

Liu, Fujiwara, Jinushi and Yamori (2016) define relationship banking as (1) banks investing in obtaining customer-specific information (soft information), often proprietary in nature; (2) firms borrowing from the same bank over time, obtaining favorable conditions, in exchange for providing soft information.

Due to the wealth of definitions for relationship banking, this paper will not establish a new one. Using the existing definitions, this paper will review the current literature by analyzing the effects, characteristics, determination of relationship banking and the new surrounding relationship banking. We also examine specifically relationship banking and SMEs.

1.2 SME Financing and Asymmetric Information

SME financing has attracted much attention in recent years, particularly after the Lehman Brothers shock in 2008. It became an important topic not only because SMEs provide employment opportunities for people in many countries, but also because the steady development of SMEs can help maintain social stability. Table 1 refers to the data from Shinozaki (2012)[2] which shows the contribution of SMEs' to the economies in Asia.[3] It

---

[1] See more details about soft and hard information in Petersen and Rajan (1994), Petersen and Rajan (2002), Berger and Udell (2002), and Stein (2002).
[2] Shinozaki (2012) also discusses a new regime of SME finance amid an era of global imbalances, with empirical analyses of bank financing for SMEs in Asian countries.
[3] See more conditions regarding SMEs in Asian countries in Shinozaki (2012).

supports the reason policymakers attach great importance to the growth of SMEs and create programs that increase lending to them and improve the operating environment of financially constrained SMEs.

Table 1. SME conditions in Asian countries

	Number of Enterprises (% of total)	Year	Number of Employees (% of total)	Year	Contribute to GDP (% of total)	Year
East Asian countries						
Japan	99.7	2006	69.4	2006	47.7	2008
Korea	99.9	2009	87.7	2009	47.6	2009
China	99.9	2008	75.0	2008	58.5	2008
South Asian countries						
Brunei Darussalam	98.4	2008	58.0	2009	22.0	2009
Cambodia	98.5	2009	-	-	85.0	2008
Indonesia	99.9	2009	97.0	2009	56.5	2009
Lao PDR	99.8	2006	83.0	2006	6 to 9	-
Malasia	99.2	2010	59.0	2010	31.9	2010
Myanmar	92.0	2007	-	-	-	-
Philippines	99.6	2009	63.2	2009	35.7	2009
Singapore	99.4	2005	62.3	2005	46.3	2005
Thailand	99.8	2010	78.2	2009	36.7	2010
Viet Nam	97.4	2007	77.3	2002	26.0	2007

Note: The data in Table 1 is from Shinozaki (2012). GDP = gross domestic product.
  The year of 2008 is used for Japan's GDP %.
  The year of 2009 is used for Philippines' GDP % with total manufacturing value added.

Furthermore, SME financing requires special attention because the informational opaqueness that characterizes SMEs makes financial difficulties far more serious for SMEs than for larger enterprises. Funding difficulties for SMEs are common not only in developing countries like China, but also in developed countries like Japan, the United States, and European countries. (Cressy (2002), Beck, Demirgü.-Kunt, (2006), Beck, Demirgü.-Kunt, and Maksimovic (2008), Vos, Yeh, Carter, and Tagg, (2007), Liu, Fujiwara, Jinushi and Yamori (2016)).

Another characteristic of SMEs is that due to the asymmetric information, SMEs can find themselves financially constrained more easily than larger firms. Asymmetric information is a more serious issue for SMEs because their financial disclosures or accounting reports are usually unclear. Asymmetric information in banking markets is generally as a phenomenon that arises from differences of information between banks and the borrowers—for example, whether borrowers can repay their loans on schedule, or if they will default, an assessment that is hard to make for banks. However, banks could avoid letting troubled borrowers (particularly SMEs) default if they built long term relationships with their borrowers. Such relationships would allow banks to gather private information about the firms; on the other hand, firms could consolidate their loans and make minimum interest payments. Relationship banking is not only important for helping banks gather private information (which reduces the cost of gathering information), but also helps firms obtain loans from financial intermediaries (Diamond (1984), Fama (1985), Lummer and McConnell (1989), Berger and Udell (2006), Cerqueiro, Degryse, and Ongena(2007)).

This paper reviews the existing literature to understand how soft information is gathered though relationship banking to help SMEs succeed in obtaining funding. The remainder of this paper is structured as follows. Section 2 describes the effects and characteristics of relationship banking. Section 3 describes the development of relationship banking for SMEs, and Section 4 concludes.

2.   The Effects and Characteristics of Relationship Banking

2.1   Reducing Costs of the Asymmetric Information

After introducing of the definitions of relationship banking, this section will summarize the empirical analysis of the effects and characteristics of relationship banking and SMEs. The data can vary depending on the country and the data sources used. For example, for American SMEs, researchers use the Survey of Small Business Finance (SSBF) which is carried out every 5~6 years. Researchers analyzing Japanese SMEs use the Survey of the Financial Environments of Small and Medium Enterprises.[4] For some countries that lack SME data sources, the studies also use listed enterprise datasets.

As mentioned in the introduction, soft information about borrowers is vitally important to financial intermediaries since not only can it mitigate the asymmetry of information, it can also reduce the costs of collecting information.[5] This is consistent with the traditional bank lending theories, which include moral hazard and adverse selection problems particularly for supplying funds to SMEs.[6] Generally speaking, SMEs do not publicize their financial status as frequently as large enterprises, because producing financial disclosures and accounting reports require much more time, manpower, and material resources for SMEs compared to larger firms (Diamond (1984), Petersen and Rajan (2002), Berger and Udell (2002)). Because of these issues of scale and information asymmetric for SMEs, strong, long-term relationships with financial intermediaries can raise the possibility of SMEs to obtain loans and lower the costs of funds.

Boot (2000) considers relationship banking to be the provision of a financial intermediary: "i) investing in obtaining customer-specific information, often proprietary in nature; and ii)

---

[4]   In Japan, the researchers also use the survey of SMEs which is supplied by the CRD (Credit Risk Database).

[5]   Overall, with a long-term relationship, both firms and banks could lower the costs of switching (between banks and firms) and also lower the costs of investing in information gathering.

[6]   In addition, a strong relationship also can improve firm performance directly through better access to banks, or reduce the agency problem through the enhanced control of banks (Rajan (1992)).

evaluating the profitability of these investments through multiple interactions with the same customer over time or products." Petersen and Rajan (1994) find that firms that build close ties with an institutional creditor will have greater access to financing. Berger and Udell (1995) establish that the bank-borrower relationship is an important mechanism for solving the problem of asymmetric information; they also find that borrowers with longer standing banking relationships paid lower interest rates and were required to pledge less collateral.

Since the global financial crisis in 2008, empirical evidence on the effects of relationship banking has focused on soft information and the changed economic environment. Presbitero and Zazzaro (2011) suggest that increased interbank competition is adverse to relationship lending in markets, while an increase in competition by a large group of small mutual banks may drive banks to further cultivate their extensive relationships with customers. Gobbi and Sette (2012) show that firms with a contraction in credit can get steadier lending and enjoy a longer relationship with financial institutions by reducing the numbers of financial institutions from which they borrow. Fraser, Ghon Rhee, and Hwan Shin (2012) find that increased capital market competition may reduce relationship lending, but that the effects differ according to the maturity of the loans. Increased capital market competition may reduce long-term relationship lending, but may increase short-term relationship lending. Uchida, Udell and Yamori (2012) argue that small banks produce more soft information with relationship lending. Bolton, Freixas, Gambacorta, and Mistrulli (2013) study how relationship lending and transaction lending vary throughout the business cycle, practically during a crisis. They find that relationship lenders charged a higher spread for their loans by gathering information about their borrowers before the crisis, and then offering more favorable lending terms to help them face the crisis, thus reducing the number of defaults.

Frazzonia, Mancusib, Rotondic and Vezzullie (2014) focus on the role of relationship banking in raising SMEs' probability of exporting. They find that the strength of the bank-firm relationship has a positive impact on both SMEs' probability of exporting and their export margins. They also discuss how bank-firm relationships supports SMEs' international activities both through financial and non-financial channels.

Beck, Degryse, Haas and Horen (2014) analyze how banks' lending techniques affect funding to SMEs over the business cycle. They collect the firm data from 21 countries and find that relationship lending has a positive impact during a downturn in the business cycle, and this result holds particularly for smaller, younger, and more opaque firms with less collateral to pledge. Similarly, Sette and Gobbi (2015) find that relationship lending mitigated the transmission of the Lehman Brothers' default shock to the supply of credit with Italian firms.

Liu, Fujiwara, Jinushi and Yamori (2016) use a unique data set from China's Zhejiang Province. They examine whether the relationship banking model can be applied to China and how relationship banking affects financing for SMEs. They accesses how Chinese SMEs can obtain financial support from banks.

2.2 Determinants of the Characteristics of Relationship Banking

2.2.1 The Duration of the Relationship

According to the definitions of relationship banking, the duration of the relationship is an important, since the longer a relationship is sustained between firms and banks, the greater the value of soft information that can be gathered, which in turn helps the relationship lasts longer. Berger and Udell (1995) determine that longer of the relationship, more practicality for firms to pay lower rates and supply less pledge collateral. Boot (2000) argues that if the relationship between lenders and borrowers lasts long enough, it may profitable for banks. There are many reports that study the length of a relationship in relationship banking. Farinha and Santos (2002) use Portuguese data on the credit filed by banks operating in Portugal with the central bank. They report that SMEs will often take out their first loan with a single bank, but afterwards they may start borrowing from additional banks. Sakai, Uesugi, and Watanabe (2010) investigate how the borrowing costs of firms decrease as they age. They find that interest rates fall as a firm's age advances and the borrower relationship lengthens.

Kim, Kristiansen, and Vale (2007) use the life cycle model of borrowing firms to test how bank-borrower relationships reduce the problems of asymmetric information and how this affects interest rates. They find that banks would provide lower interest rates for younger firms, but when firms surpassed the 10-year relationship mark, banks tend to increase the interest rates they charge. This may be indicative of the hold-up problem. Only when a firm reaches 40 years of age does the bank lower its interest rate again. This suggests that the problem of information asymmetry depends on the firm's age.

Ongena and Smith (2001) use panel data from Norway and find that the relationship between firms and banks varies from 15~18 years. Angelini, Di Salvo, and Ferri (1998) report a mean relationship length of 14 years in Italy. For American relationships, Cole (1998) and Petersen and Rajan (1994) report 7 years and 11 years, respectively. Elsas and Krahnen (1998) find 22 years to be common in Germany. Uchida, Udell, and Watanebe (2008) observe 32~33 years long relationship in Japan, while Degryse and Van Cayseele (2000) find them to be 8 years in Belgium, and Liu, Fujiwara, Jinushi and Yamori (2016) note about 5 years in China.

2.2.2 Number of Financial Intermediaries and Multiple Relationships

Compared to larger firms, smaller firms tend to maintain fewer banking relationships

(Degryse, Kim, and Ongena (2008)).[7] Degryse, Kim and Ongena (2008) also argue that the firms that are order find it easier to maintain many relationships with banks. Rajan (1992)[8] point out that the higher the numbers of relationships that banks have with firms, the lower risk for the hold-up problems.[9] Detragiache, Garella, and Guiso (2000) study the determinants of the number of bank-lending relationships with SMEs in Italy, and find that the number of bank relationships is based on the behavior of the bank. Firms increase the numbers of relationship banks for two reasons: (1) to share their risk and (2) banks aim to maximize their number of customers.

2.3   The Costs of Relationship Banking

As many studies point out, relationship banking comes at a cost. Boot (2000) identifies two primary costs of relationship banking: the soft budget problem and the hold-up problem. The soft budget problem refers to the fact that, as a bank cannot deny additional credit to a borrower with whom they maintain a close relationship, when the firm falls into a situation of financial difficulty, the bank will keep inefficient borrowers afloat. As so-called zombie firms continue to obtain funds, the efficiency of the economy deteriorates (Liu, Fujiwara, Jinushi and Yamori (2016)).

Another issue is the hold-up problem.[10] Sharpe (1990) argues that banks use the power of the information monopoly to build their reputations, which leads to higher costs for customers and the hold-up issue. He also points out that long term banking relationships arise in completive loan markets because banks may offer only above-cost loans to their long term customers while holding up customers from the other banks.

Greenbaum, Kanatas, and Venezia (1989) argue that banks collect soft information through the provision of financial services to firms over a long period of time. They then charge interest rates that maximize their profits, because they know that borrowers cannot turn to other lenders that have no soft information about them. Accordingly, borrowers are forced to pay higher interest rates. The hold-up problem is also present in Rajan (1992), which finds that banks have bargaining power based on the long-term borrower relationship, and can decide how firms finance new projects. Firms cannot choose low-cost funds without the bank's permission, which

---

[7]   For example, American studies using the National Survey of Small Business Finance find that the mean number of banks used by SMEs is between one and two.

[8]   Rajan (1992) also notes that because of information asymmetries, relationships between banks and firms arise endogenously even in competitive loan markets, which is consistent with Sharper (1990).

[9]   See Section 2.3 for an explanation of the holdup problem in relationship banking.

[10]   Following Berger and Udell (1995), many studies discuss the costs of credit and all types of costs associated with firms'. However, there are no clear results about why holdup problems for customers should apply to one class of loans only.

results in costly financing. Degryse and Cayseele (2000) find that firms that have longer relationships with fewer banks tend to pay higher loan rates, but firms that borrow from more banks are required to pledge less collateral. Ongena and Smith (2001) compare the number of banking relationships held by firms. They find that firms that have relationships with multiple banks reduce the risk of being held up by banks, while firms that have long-term relationships with only one bank can more easily be locked in with their lenders.

3.   The Development of Relationship Banking and SMEs

As mentioned above, since the global financial crisis of 2008, empirical evidence on the effects of relationship banking has focused on soft information and how the changed financial economic environment affects the relationship banking, especially in the case of SMEs.
Railienė (2014) argues that relationship banking has changed since the 2008 crisis as a result of the distinct change in two conditions, information technology (IT) and the economic environment, thus affecting the value of soft information. In this paper, we note that the recent financial crisis has taught us about how the development of IT caused the nature of relationship banking to change. We also observe that the dimensions related to the valuation of relationship banking are closely related to service quality measures. "While reasoning on relationship banking in light of IT use and distance, the e-service quality measures are addressed. The major fields measured in e-service quality of finance institutions are trust, customised communications, ease of use, website content and functionality, reliability and speed of delivery (Changsoo & Suresh, 2008)."

Everett (2015) uses a new data source, online social lending (peer-to-peer lending), to study the impact of borrower-lender information asymmetries, moral hazard, and the holdup problem. These changes may mean that, in the near future, relationship banking may require new definitions, not only between the firms (or SMEs) and financial intermediaries, but also between online financial intermediaries (including private financial businesses) and new forms of lending which depend on financial technology (FinTech).

4.   Conclusion

This paper discusses the development of relationship banking. According to both the earlier literatures (Diamond (1984), Petersen and Rajan (1994, 1995), Berger and Udell (1995), Boot (2000), Berger and Udell (2002)) and recent theoretical papers, relationship banking, especially in the case of SMEs, is an important area of research. The strength of a firm's relationship with banks can be measured by the duration of the relationship over time, and by the number of financial intermediaries with whom they work.

Relationship banking have many benefits for firms, and particularly for SMEs. For example, it can help a firm obtain loans at lower rates, allow SMEs to obtain funding even in the downturn of a business cycle, support the firms' international activities, and also can reduce the costs of producing information for both firms and financial intermediaries. On the other hand, relationship banking is associate with the soft budget problem and the hold-up problem (Boot (2000)). However, the changes in information technology (IT) and the economic environment since the 2008 financial crisis have also shifted the nature of relationship banking. More research is needed on this topic, particularly in the new financial environment. While many studies have examined American, Japanese and European cases, other countries in Asian, Africa, counties and other developing countries need more examination about relationship banking and SMEs.

Acknowledgments

The author wishes to thank Professor Kadoya and Professor Teramoto of Hiroshima Shudo University for their research support for this paper. She also wishes to thank Professor Yamori, Professor Jinushi, and Professor Fujiwara of Kobe University for their useful comments. The author is also grateful to Jane Imai, for her constructive comments which improved the article.

References

[1] Angelini, P., Di Salvo, R., and Ferri, G. (1998). Availability and Cost of Credit for Small Businesses: Customer Relationships and Credit Cooperatives, *Journal of Banking and Finance*, 22, 925–954.

[2] Beck, T., Demirgü.-Kunt, A., Maksimovic, V. (2005). Financial and legal constraints to firm growth: Does firm size matter. *Journal of Finance,* 60, 137–177.

[3] Beck, T., Demirgü.-Kunt, A. (2006). Small and medium-size enterprises: Access to finance as a growth constraint. *Journal of Banking and Finance*, 30, 2931–2943.

[4] Beck, T., Demirgü.-Kunt, A., Maksimovic, V. (2008). Financing patterns around the world: Are small firms different. *Journal of Financial Economics,* 89, 467–487.

[5] Beck, T., Degryse, H., Haas, R.D., Horen, N. (2014). When arm's length is too far. Relationship banking over the business cycle, BOFIT Discussion Papers 14.

[6] Berger, A. N. and Udell, G. F. (1995). Relationship Lending and Lines of Credit in Small Firm Finance*, Journal of Business*, 68, 351–381.

[7] Berger, A. N. and Udell, G. F. (2002). Small Business Credit Availability and Relationship Lending: The Importance of Bank Organizational Structure, The Economic Journal, 112, F32–F53.

[8] Berger, A. N. and Udell, G. F. (2006). A More Complete Conceptual Framework for SME Finance, *Journal of Banking and Finance*, 30, 613–673.

[9] Bolton, P., Freixas, X., Gambacorta, L., Mistrulli, P.E (2013). Relationship and Transaction Lending in a Crisis, Temi di Discussione 917, Bank of Italy.

[10] Boot, A. W. A. (2000). Relationship Banking: What Do We Know? *Journal of Financial Intermediation*, 9, 7–25.

[11] Cerqueiro, G., Degryse, H., Ongena, S. (2007), Distance, bank organizational structure and credit, Discussion papers.

[12] Changsoo, S., & Suresh, K. T. (2008). Development of e-service quality measure for internet-based financial institutions, *Journal of Total Quality Management & Business Excellence*, 19, 903-918.

[13] Cole, Rebel A. (1998). The Importance of Relationships to the Availability of Credit, *Journal of Banking and Finance,* 22, 1998, pp. 959–977.

[14] Cressy, R. (2002). Funding gaps: A symposium. *Economic Journal,* 112, 1–16.

[15] Degrys, H., Ongena, S. (2008). Competition and Regulation in the Banking Sector: A Review of the Empirical Evidence on the Sources of Bank Rents, Handbook of financial intermediation and banking, 483–554.

[16] Detragiache, Enrica, Garella, P., Guiso, L. (2000). Multiple versus Single Banking Relationships: Theory and Evidence, *Journal of Finance,* 55, 1133–1161.

[17] Diamond, D. W. (1984). Financial Intermediation and Delegated Monitoring, *Review of Economic Studies*, LI, 393–414.

[18] Elsas, R., Krahnen, J. P. (1998). Is Relationship Lending Special? Evidence From Credit-File Data in Germany, *Journal of Banking Finance*, 22, 1283–1316.

[19] Everett, Craig R. (2015). Group Membership, Relationship Banking and Loan Default Risk: The Case of Online Social Lending. *Banking and Finance Review*, 7(2).

[20] Fama, E.F. (1985). What's different about banks? Journal of monetary economics, 15, 29-39.

[21] Farinha, Luísa A., João A. C. Santos. (2002). Switching from Single to Multiple Bank Lending Relationships: Determinants and Implications, *Journal of Financial Intermediation*, 11, 124–151.

[22] Fraser, D.R., Rhee, S. G., Shin, G.H. (2012). The Impact of Capital Market Competition on Relationship Banking: Evidence from the Japanese Experience, *Journal of Empirical Finance*, 19, 411-426.

[23] Frazzoni, S., Mancusi, M. L., Rotondi, Z., Maurizio Sobrero, Vezzulli, A. (2014). Innovation and export in SMEs: the role of relationship banking, Working Paper n. 18

[24] Gobbi, G., and E. Sette. (2012). Relationship Lending in a Financial Turmoil, Mo.Fi.R. Working Paper, No. 59, Marche Polytechnic University, Ancona.

[25] Greenbaum, S. I., Kanatas, G., and Venezia, I. (1989). Equilibrium Loan Pricing under the Bank-Client Relationship, *Journal of Banking Finance*, 13, 221–235.

[26] Kim, M., Kristiansen, E. G., Vale, B. (2007). Life-Cycle Patterns of Interest Rate Markups in Small Firm Finance, Norges Bank Working Paper.

[27] Liu, Y. J., Fujiwara, K., Jinushi, T., Yamori, N. (2016). How should banks support SMEs to manage funding risks in China? The Role of Relationship Banking. Risk Management in Emerging Markets: Issues, Framework and Modeling, 363-396.

[28] Lummer, S.L., McConnell, J.J. (1989). Further evidence on the bank lending process and the capital-market response to bank loan agreements, *Journal of financial economics*, 25, 99-122.

[29] Ongena, S., Smith, D. (1998). Quality and Duration of Bank Relationships, *Global Cash Management in Europe*, 224–235

[30] Ongena, S., Smith, D. (2001). The Duration of Bank Relationships, *Journal of Financial Economics,* 61, 449–475.

[31] Petersen, M. A. and Rajan, R. G. (1994). The Benefits of Lending Relationships: Evidence from Small Business Data, *The Journal of Finance*, 49, 3–37.

[32] Petersen, M. A. and Rajan, R. G. (1995). The Effect of Credit Market Competition on Lending Relationships, *Quarterly Journal of Economics*, 110, 406–443.

[33] Petersen, M. A. and Rajan, R. G. (2002). Does Distance Still Matter? The Information Revolution in Small Business Lending, *The Journal of Finance*, 57, 2533–2570.

[34] Presbitero, A and Zazzaro, A. (2011). Competition and Relationship Lending: Friends or Foes? *Journal of Financial Intermediation,* 20, 387–413.

[35] Railienė, G. (2014). The Use of IT in Relationship Banking, *Procedia – Social and Behavioral Sciences*, 156, 569–574.

[36] Rajan, R. G. (1992). Insiders and Outsiders: The Choice Between Informed and Arm's-Length Debt, *The Journal of Finance*, 47, 1367–1400.

[37] Sakai, K., Uesugi, I., Watanabe, T. (2010). Firm Age and the Evolution of Borrowing Costs: Evidence from Japanese Small Firms, *Journal of Banking and Finance*, 34, 1970–1981.

[38] Sette, E., Gobbi, G. (2015). Relationship Lending During a Financial Crisis, *Journal of the European Economic Association*, 13, 453–481.

[39] Shinozaki, Shigehiro (2012) : A New Regime of SME Finance in Emerging Asia: Empowering Growth-Oriented SMEs to Build Resilient National Economies, ADB Working Paper Series on Regional Economic Integration, No. 104.

[40] Stein, Jeremy C. (2002). Information production and capital allocation: Decentralized vs. hierarchical firms, *The Journal of Finance*, 57,1891–1921.

[41] Uchida, H., Udell, G., and Yamori, N. (2008). How do Japanese Banks Discipline Small and Medium-Sized Borrowers? An Investigation of the Deployment of Lending Technologies, *International Finance Review (Institutional Approach to Global Corporate Governance)*, 9, 57–80.

[42] Uchida, H., Udell, G., and Yamori, N. (2012). Loan Officers and Relationship Lending to SMEs, *Journal of financial Intermediation*, 21, 97-122.

[43] Vos, E., Yeh, A.J., Carter, S., Tagg, S. (2007). The happy story of small business financing, *Journal of Banking and Finance*, 31, 2648–2672.

Chapter 7

Considering the Personality Development of Project Managers: Proposal of a PM Report Card

Tatsuo Sato

Faculty of Economic Sciences, Hiroshima Shudo University

1-1 Ozuka-Higashi 1-chome, Asaminami-ku, Hiroshima, Japan 731-3195

Abstract

Personality is an important trait for a project manager (PM), yet it is difficult to develop effective programs for personality development. Overemphasis on the importance of PM's personality may make it difficult to develop those who work in this role. This paper discusses effective personality development of PMs and proposes a novel PM Report Card as an effective means of fostering development.

Key Words:

Project manager (PM), Personality development, Report card

1. Introduction

Japan's information technology (IT) industry at the start of 2000 had experienced many failed projects, and development of project manager (PM) was seen as an important issue underlying this reality. *A Guide to the Project Management Body of Knowledge (PMBOK® Guide)* published by the US Project Management Institute appeared to be something of a savior for Japan's IT industry, and rapidly penetrated the entire industry. Many IT companies introduced development programs using the *PMBOK® Guide* to assist with PM development policies. Then, *Project Management Competency Development Frameworks (PMCDF®)*, published as a function development system based on the *PMBOK® Guide* defined knowledge, practice, and personality as three elements necessary in developing PM. With this, the flow for developing project management technology skills to acquire knowledge (scope, time, cost, quality, human resources, communication, risk, procurement, stakeholders) at the desk and practice learning outcomes in actual projects was established. However, effective methods have not been found for developing PM's personality. This paper organizes the problems in such development and proposes a PM Report Card as an effective guideline toward a solution.

2.   Problem Definition

There are certain problems and solutions in developing PM's personality.

2.1   Problems in Fostering the Personality of PM

Three particular points of concern are noted as problems in this development.

1) Does PM possess an outstanding personality?

Many PMs are portrayed in the media as elite-level individuals who combine high technological proficiency and outstanding personality. Indeed, many difficult projects cannot succeed without a highly capable PM who possesses such a personality. But do many companies now actually need such elite individuals? Before such goals are attainted, it is important to develop PMs who can perform basic actions. When considering the size and difficulty of a project in a company it is important to clarify the aptitudes PM will provide. This helps in developing a clear portrait of PM the company must develop.

2) Is it impossible to provide education for PM's personality?

It often said that personality does not change during one's education, and that people with effective personalities can be selected. Personality is undoubtedly greatly affected by innate influences such as congenital traits or upbringing; therefore, certain traits may be unchangeable at a later stage. However, those who acquire the necessary leadership skills for project management did not necessarily possess them from the outset. Rather, they gradually went through various experiences and grew to become PMs. Education should be used to train the personality traits PM needs.

3) Can personality be evaluated?

With regard to the degree of acquisition of knowledge, PM's technical abilities can be evaluated by means such as tests. Practical skills can be evaluated by visible output such as what was created in actual projects, but personality has no visible output. It is difficult to evaluate something that cannot be seen; this is one reason personality is not actively developed. However, if one can visualize the personality of PM, one can evaluate it.

2.2   Solutions to Problems

There are three notable solutions to the aforementioned problems.

1) Clarify the targets of PM's development

In my personal experience, the number of people of whom one project PM can gain a strong understanding is about 10. With sub-PMs or team leaders, this can be extended to about 20. Any more than that will be difficult to manage. A manager of a large project can look at the entire project via the lower-level leaders, and in this case as well, about 10 people can be effectively managed.

The ability to manage such as project, of about 10 people, is fundamental. This corresponds to level 4 of the Skill Standards for IT Professionals (ITSS) defined by the Information-technology Promotion Agency (IPA) of Japan [1] (Table 1).

Table 1. PM levels based on Skill Standards for IT Professionals (ITSS)

Level	Size
Level 7	More than 500 project members at peak hours or annual contract amount more than 1 billion yen
Level 6	More than 50 project members at peak hours or annual contract amount more than 500 million yen
Level 5	More than 10 project members at peak hours or annual contract amount less than 500 million yen
Level 4	Less than 10 project members at peak hours or annual contract amount less than 100 million yen
Level 3	Participate in project as project member

Source: Skill Standards for IT Professionals (ITSS) V3, IPA (2011) [1]

Emphasis should be placed on developing a person to this basic level prior to thinking about choosing an outstanding PM.

2) Evaluate concrete actions

As mentioned, personality has no visible output. For example, even if one says, "You need to acquire leadership skills" or "You are lacking leadership ability," it is not clear what exactly needs to be improved. It is impossible for evaluators to explain the needs concretely.

This is because leadership is a general term for actions leading to various situations in a project; leadership does not concretely exist, and one cannot evaluate such a thing. Therefore, to nurture leadership, it is necessary to evaluate concrete actions PM performed in leading projects in various situations, and provide specific guidance to give that person awareness.

Do not use the expression personality to encompass all individual behaviors, but instead clearly show each person's problems and improvement points by observing, evaluating, and guiding each of them toward concrete actions. Repeating this leads to education for personality development.

3) Clarify the perspective and scale of evaluation

It is effective to observe specific actions and evaluate and instruct on them to develop PM's personality. However, it is difficult to objectively evaluate human behavior such as in project plans, schedules, or other such output. There is a degree of uncertainty in that the evaluation depends on the thinking and experience of the evaluator.

Evaluation items can mitigate differences among evaluators by listing concrete actions classified under PM leadership and clearly indicating viewpoints and scales of evaluation. It is important to increase the evaluation's validity by having multiple experts, such as experienced veteran PMs and others responsible for training PMs and Project Management Office (PMO) personnel, create the criteria.

3.   Proposal of PM Report Card

I have previously advocated that for topics without established solutions, such as development of PMs, it is effective to apply cases from other fields, and that have already been proven [2].

In considering a mechanism to develop PM's personality, this paper looks to Japanese elementary school report cards. These report cards, familiar to anyone schooled in Japan, are a tool for nurturing personal attributes. Elementary school education in Japan aims not to select outstanding individuals but rather to observe students' behavior and enhance it through evaluation and guidance. Standards are set in accordance with the guidelines of the Ministry of Education, Culture, Sports, Science and Technology of Japan [3] (Figure 1). This approach can be sufficiently applied to develop personality of PM.

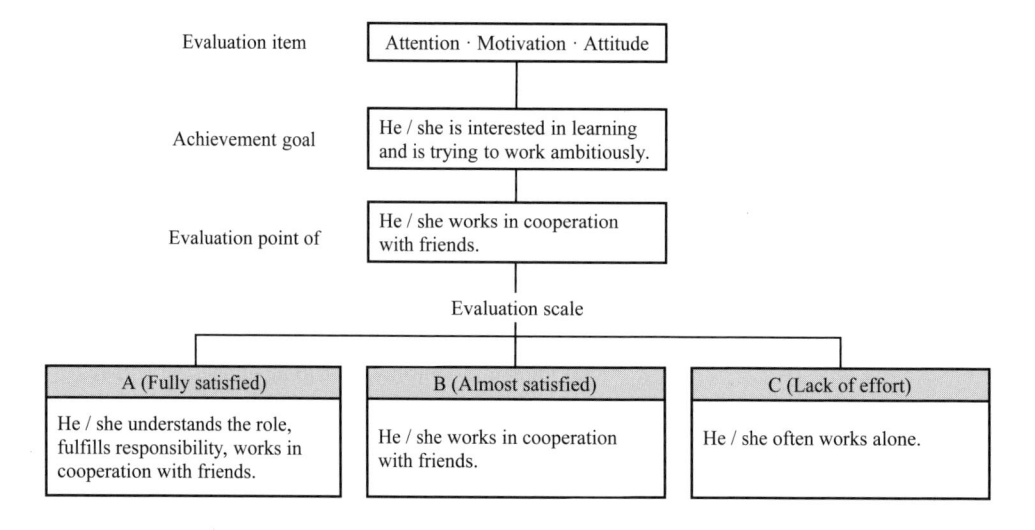

Figure 1.   Evaluation items of a Japanese elementary school report card (example). Created with reference to [3].

3.1   Outline of PM Report Card

The PM Report Card summarizes project PMs' specific actions in various scenarios of a project, and the viewpoints and scales of evaluation for it, to develop PMs' personalities (Table 2).

Table 2. Example of PM Report Card

Evaluation item	Evaluation point of view	Evaluation scale		
		A (Fully satisfied)	B (Almost satisfied)	C (Lack of effort)
PM leads the project members at the meeting.	PM had started the meeting on time.	PM called for all members to start the meeting on time.	PM entered the meeting room ahead of time and was meeting on time.	The meeting did not start even after hours.
	PM aggressively managed the meeting.	PM knew the agenda beforehand and was aware of time allocation.	PM sat in the center of the meeting room and managed the meeting.	PM did not sit in the center of the meeting room and did not know who managed the meeting.
	PM used the meeting effectively as a place of information exchange.	PM positively heard to the opinions of the members and also showed my ideas.	PM was about to hear the opinions of the members.	The meeting was not an effective opportunity.
	PM timely responded to the ploblemss reported at the meeting.	PM decided the deadline for the problems solving and confirmed the progress situation.	PM was trying to take action to solve the problems.	PM had neglected the problems.
	PM had finished the meeting on time.	PM had finished the meeting on time and had dissolved it after confirming the decisions and pending items, homework.	PM was trying to end the meeting on time.	PM had been discussing even though time passed.

1) Evaluation items

These items parse out the personality of PM to action levels, such as desirable behavior for PM to demonstrate leadership.

2) Evaluation perspective

These specific actions further subdivide the evaluation items. By documenting the daily actions of PM, the vague aspects of personality become more concrete.

3) Evaluation scale

This is an index for evaluation and guidance. Using it for concrete feedback permits improvement of insufficient areas and maintenance and strengthening of what is being done well.

3.2   Flow of evaluation and guidance through PM Report Card

There is a flow of evaluation and guidance when using the PM Report Card (Figure 2).

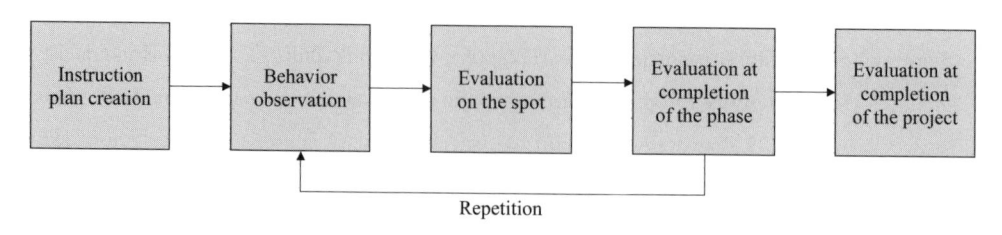

Figure 2.   Instruction and evaluation flow through PM Report Card

1) Preparation of PM development plan

When PM starts a project with a target, the evaluator creates a development plan in unison with a project implementation plan, and sets the achievement goals in consideration of PM's shortcomings.

2) Evaluate behavior

The evaluator observes the actual behavior in the project activity and conducts the evaluation in line with the items on the PM Report Card.

3) Evaluate on the spot

Evaluators do not evaluate collectively and retrospectively, but instead do so by giving feedback on the spot. This provides the recipient with awareness.

4) Guidance upon completion of project phase

Evaluations are given on the spot. However, feedback is also given retrospectively, such as upon completion of the project phase, in the PM Report Card to compel PM toward achieving the targets, leading to improvements in the next phase.

5) Evaluate upon project completion

The degree of accomplishment is fed back in line with the growth target, using the Report Card in unified timing with the project completion report. In this way, PM can again recognize strong points in actions taken in charge of projects, along with points in need of improvement. These can be used and applied for action in the next project.

3.3   Evaluation of PM Report Card

Through evaluation of PMs targeted for developing using the PM Report Card, in observing PM's daily behavior, superiors who are evaluators can pinpoint those suited for higher positions. However, superiors must have abundant knowledge and experience in project management, possess strong leadership abilities, and be able to evaluate calmly and objectively.

PMO staff are also involved. They must attend project meetings and visit the project, site to observe, evaluate, and give instruction on the behavior of PM targeted for training. PMO personnel are in the position to objectively evaluate the project, thereby enabling evaluation of PM's behavior.

Whether to make a leader a higher manager or PMO staff will vary depending on the company's structure, but in either case it is important to have knowledge, experience, and leadership in project management. Fairness and appraisal of the evaluation should also be ensured based on the PM Report Card.

4. Expected Effects

The expected effects of the PM Report Card are as follows.

1) Provide specific evaluation and guidance through clarification of evaluation criteria

With respect to personality, which, as mentioned, has been something that could not be visualized, by focusing on PM's actual actions and clarifying the evaluation's perspectives and its scale for the action, specific items for evaluation and guidance become possible, and not merely subjective.

2) Provide awareness through on-site evaluation and guidance

By giving evaluation and guidance on the spot, rather than collecting and giving feedback retrospectively, PM will be able to immediately realize good or bad actions, which greater enables improvement to be made. Additionally, by again feeding back through the PM Report Card upon phase and project completion, retrospective encouragement is possible and the guidance can be applied at the next opportunity.

3) Realize growth by setting targets

Growth targets should be set at the start of the project. Skills can be heightened, while realizing growth, by repeating the cycle of receiving feedback-based guidance in evaluations at each stage in the project period and by PM making realizations and subsequently improving.

5. Conclusion

This paper proposes a PM Report Card, inspired by Japanese elementary school report cards and their communications, that can be used to develop PM's personality. This does not imply PMs should be trained at the same level as elementary school students, rather it is an attempt to solve problems in PM development by applying an effective case from another field analogously.

In the future, it will be important to improve the evaluation items and apply them in actuality. I hope to be able to promote this mechanism in the workplace.

References

[1] Information-technology Promotion Agency, Japan (IPA), "Skill Standards for IT Professionals V3" (2011) http://www.ipa.go.jp/jinzai/itss/download_V3_2011.html (Reference; September 20, 2017)

[2] Sato, T. and Ito, H., "Project manager development method" (in Japanese), JUSE Press (2006)

[3] Suzuki, S., "Absolute evaluation practice manual for elementary school teachers" (in Japanese), Gakuyo Shobo (2002)

Contributors

Chris Czerkawski, *Professor, Hiroshima Shudo University*

Ph.D. in International Economics. Currently with Faculty of Economic Sciences, Hiroshima Shudo University. Previously teaching at Griffith University, Brisbane Australia and Edith Cowan University in Perth Australia. Research interests include foreign exchange markets, new financial markets in Asia Pacific area. Main teaching areas include International Finance, International Financial Management, International Economics.

Osamu KURIHARA, *Visiting Proffesor, Hiroshima University*

A visiting professor in Hiroshima University. He was educated at Meiji Gakuin University, Hiroshima University and Hiroshima Shudo University where he completed his PhD. He was a professor at the Faculty of Contemporary Sociology in Hiroshima Kokusai-Gakuin University from 2006 to 2016. He mainly lectures Macroeconomics and International Economics in several Universities. And he is also a priest of Jodo Shinshu Hongwanji-ha.

His research interests are Balance of Payments, Exchange rates and capital flows, currently and historically. He has been a director in Japan Academy for International Trade and Business from 2009.

Hiroyuki DEKIHARA, *Associate Professor, Hiroshima Shudo University*

Hiroyuki Dekihara is an associate professor at the Faculty of Economic Sciences in Hiroshima Shudo University, where he has been since 2017. He received his Ph.D. in Information Engineering from Hiroshima City University, Japan, in 2003. From 2001 to 2016, he worked at Hiroshima International University, eventually as an associate professor. His research interests span both C/S systems and data engineering. Much of his work has been on improving and developing mechanism of server that manages clients. He presented at a paper titled "An Extended Technique for R-tree to Manage Multiple Type Objects", Journal of Computational Methods in Sciences and Engineering, Vol.12, pp.S53-S61(2012). Currently, he is a member of research project developing educational frameworks and contents on key technologies of Forth Industrial Revolution: AI, IoT, Virtualization, etc.

Tatsuya IWAKI, *Professor, Hiroshima International University*

He received his Ph.D. from Hiroshima University, Japan. He is a Professor at Faculty of

Rehabilitation, Hiroshima International University, Japan. He primarily studies human emotion and its temporal dynamics, using psychophysiological and affective-engineering approaches.

Nan ZHANG, *Professor, Hiroshima Shudo University*

He is a professor of statistics in the Faulty of Economic Sciences. He received his Ph.D. in Economics from Ritsumeikan University in 1993, and then he has been working in Hiroshima Shudo University since 1995. He has ever worked as visiting scholar in East Asian Institute at Columbia University (2001-2002), the Department of Statistics at University of California, Berkeley (2007-2008), and the Department of Statistics at Stanford University (2014-2015). As a contribution to the international community, he has been named a Technical Assistance Expert by the Statistics Department of the IMF since 2008. His research focuses on Global Flow of Funds Analysis, Monetary & Financial Statistics and Economic Statistics. His major publications are as follows. The Flow of Funds Analysis in Theory and Practice: Statistics Observations on the Flow of Funds in China (Peking University Press, 2014), The Global Flow of Funds Analysis in Theory and Application (Minerva Shobo, 2005), The Flow-of-Funds Analysis in Theory and Practice (Minerva-shobo, 1996) etc. In addition, many papers published in academic journals such as Statistics, Quantitative & Technical Economics, Statistical Research, Journal of Data Analysis etc.

Ryoko WADA, *Professor, Hiroshima Shudo University*

Ryoko Wada is a Professor at the Faculty and Graduate School of Economic Sciences of Hiroshima Shudo University. She received the Doctor Degree of Science from Sophia University, Japan, in 1988. Her major research areas are harmonic analysis on homogeneous spaces. Especially she is engaged in topics on integral representations of harmonic polynomials.

Yoshio AGAOKA, *Professor, Hiroshima University*

Yoshio Agaoka is a Professor at the Graduate School of Science of Hiroshima University. He graduated from Kyoto University (Faculty of Science) in 1977, and entered the Graduate School of Science, received the Doctor Degree of Science from Kyoto University in 1985. His major research areas are Differential Geometry, Representation Theory and Discrete Geometry. Especially he is engaged in topics on local isometric imbeddings of Riemannian symmetric spaces, decomposition formula of plethysms and classification of tilings of the two-dimensional sphere, etc. Recently, he is mainly engaged in the subject on elementary geometry from the viewpoint of classical invariant theory.

Setsuko SAKAI, *Professor, Hiroshima Shudo University*

Setsuko Sakai graduated from the Faculty of Education, Fukui University, 1979. She finished her doctoral course of Informatics and Mathematical Science at Osaka University in 1984. She became a lecturer at the College of Business Administration and In-formation Science, Koshien University, in 1986, and then an associate professor of the Faculty of Education, Fukui University, in 1990. Since 1998, she has been with the Faculty of Commercial Sciences of Hiroshima Shudo University, where she is a professor in the Department of Business Administration. She is currently working on game theory, decision making, nonlinear optimization by using direct search methods, evolutionary computation, swarm intelligence and fuzzy mathematical programming. She is a member of the Operations Research Society of Japan, Japan Society for Fuzzy Theory and Intelligent Informatics, and the Japan Society for Production Management. She holds a D.Eng. degree. She has published papers such as "Tuning fuzzy control rules by α con-strained method which solves constrained nonlinear optimization problems" (1999) and "Reducing the Number of Function Evaluations in Differential Evolution by Estimated Comparison Method using an Approximation Model with Low Accuracy"(2008) in The Transactions of the Institute of Electronics, Information and Communication Engineers, "Fast and Stable Constrained Optimization by the ε Constrained Differential Evolution" in Pacific Journal of Optimization (2009) and so on. She has also published papers in such journals as IEEE Transactions on Evolutionary Computation, Journal of Optimization Theory and its Applications, Transactions of the Japanese Society for Artificial Intelligence etc.

Tetsuyuki TAKAHAMA, *Professor, Hiroshima City University*

Tetsuyuki Takahama graduated from the Department of Electrical Engineering II, Kyoto University, in 1982. He finished his doctoral course in 1987. He became an assistant professor, and then a lecturer, at Fukui University in 1994. Since 1998, he has been with the Faculty of Information Science of Hiroshima City University, where he is an associate professor in the Department of Intelligent Systems. He is currently working on natural computing including evolutionary computation and swarm intelligence, nonlinear optimization and machine learning. He is a member of the Information Processing Society of Japan, the Japan Society for Artificial Intelligence, the Japanese Society of Information and Systems in Education, the Association for Natural Language Processing and IEEE. He holds a D.Eng. degree. He has published papers such as "Structural Optimization by Genetic Algorithm with Degeneration (GA^d)" in The Transactions of the Institute of Electronics, Information and Communication Engineers (2003). "Constrained Optimization by Applying the α Constrained Method to the Nonlinear Simplex Method with Mutations" in IEEE Transactions on Evolutionary Computation (2005). "Efficient Constrained Optimization by the ε Constrained Differential Evolution Using an Approximation

Model with Low Accuracy" in Transactions of the Japanese Society for Artificial Intelligence (2009) and so on. He has also published papers in such journals as Information Processing Society of Japan Journal, International Journal of Innovative Computing, Information and Control Journal of Japan Society for Fuzzy Theory and Systems etc.

Yajing LIU, *Assistant Professor, Hiroshima Shudo University*

Yajing Liu is an assistant professor at Faculty of Economic Sciences, Hiroshima Shudo University. She is also a researcher at the Graduate School of Economics, Kobe University. She received a Master's degree in 2012 and a Ph.D in 2015 from the Graduate School of Economics at Kobe University. Her research is focused on small and medium enterprise finance in China. She also does comparative research on small and medium enterprise finance between China and other countries, such as Japan. She is a member of the Japan Society of Monetary Economics, and she peer reviews articles with the Singapore Economic Review and Emerging Markets Finance and Trade. She published academic articles in journals, such as Risk Management in Emerging Markets: Issues, Framework and Modeling and Japanese Journal of Monetary and Financial Economics.

Tatsuo SATO, *Associate Professor, Hiroshima Shudo University*

Tatsuo Sato is an associate professor at the Faculty of Economic Science in Hiroshima Shudo University, and he has lectured on "Project Management" and"Design Thinking" since 2016. He received Ph.D. from Tokyo University of Agriculture and Technology in 2014. His major research areas are project management theory. Especially he has been studying value creation type project management model.

Series of Monographs of Contemporary Social Systems Solutions
Produced by
the Faculty of Economic Sciences, Hiroshima Shudo University

190 × 265 mm   5,000 yen (tax not included)

Volume 1   Social Systems Solutions by Legal Informatics, Economic Sciences and Computer Sciences

Edited by Munenori Kitahara and Kazunori Morioka   160 pages   ISBN 978-4-7985-0011-9

Volume 2   The New Viewpoints and New Solutions of Economic Sciences in the Information Society

Edited by Shusaku Hiraki and Nan Zhang   160 pages   ISBN 978-4-7985-0055-3

Volume 8 Challenging Researches in Economic Sciences: Legal Informatics, Environmental Economics, Economics, OR and Mathematics

Edited by Munenori Kitahara and Hiroaki Teramoto   152 pages ISBN 978-4-7985-0206-9